MW01623654

Better Homes and Gardens®

celebrate the SEASON® 2012

contents

In Memoriam: E.T. Meredith III (1933–2003)

Des Moines, Iowa.
First Edition.

Printed in the United States of America.
ISSN: 10980733 ISBN: 978-0-696-30111-7

Giving

I absolutely love looking forward to the holiday season. Sometimes I think the planning is almost as much fun as the holidays themselves.

What can I serve? Whom should I invite? What gifts will I make? How can I surprise someone? When should I host my party? How will I decorate? The lists go on and on.

Sometimes those lists can seem a bit overwhelming. Even when we have the best of intentions, time seems to slip away. On occasion we say, "next year," and surrender to the fact that we can't always check everything off our holiday to-do lists as we'd like. That's where *Celebrate the Season* steps in.

Need a get-together guru? Rely on us to give you not only the best kitchen-tested recipes but also festive table settings and party favors to make every Thanksgiving, Christmas, and New Year's gathering extraordinary.

On the lookout for perfect gift ideas? We give you ideas for handcrafted presents your family and friends will absolutely treasure.

Want to transform your home into a winter wonderland? Look no further for bright ideas to create everything from wreaths and centerpieces to ornaments, stockings, package wraps, and so much more.

Yes, the holiday season opens a world of opportunity for each of us to give generously of ourselves. It's our hope that the recipes, projects, and ideas in *Celebrate the Season* help to make this year a little less stressful and a lot more unforgettable for you and yours.

Wishing you all the season's best gifts,

Sue Barker

fall

Capture the flavor of fall with delightful home decorations showcasing the glorious colors and textures of the season.

Details, Details

Give a plain wooden box a glorious facelift with the addition of pressed-wood medallions. Available at crafts stores, medallions can be purchased in many sizes and motifs. Choose those that fit the box and use wood glue and small clamps to affix them. When dry, remove the clamps and stain the entire box using the desired color of wood stain. When dry, follow with a clear topcoat.

Wooden Wonders

Natural wood, brought to life with enriching stains, brings a touch of elegance to autumn decorating.

Pure Patchwork

Decorative squares line up easily to frame a tile, mirror, or photo. Start with eight 4-inch-square wooden rosettes and a 12-inch square of ⅛-inch plywood. Stain the top and sides of all wood squares; let dry. Top-coat with clear polyurethane. Use wood glue to adhere the decorative wood squares to the back piece. Use strong adhesive to attach the tile. Let glue dry.

Grand Stand

A bun foot, normally used in sets of four under furniture, stands solo as a stunning candleholder. To bring out the wood grain, stain the wood piece to the desired color, let dry, and top-coat with clear polyurethane. When dry, glue a circle of felt to the bottom. To protect wood from wax drippings, place a candle plate on top before lighting the candle.

Center of Attention

Natural tones and textures are key to these brilliant fall centerpieces.

Cup O' Plenty

A tall coffee mug, in autumnal colors, does double duty as a vase. Fill it with fall flowers backed with wispy wheat stalks for a creative last-minute arrangement.

Floral Cornucopia

In lieu of fruit, fill a cornucopia with a fresh bouquet. To keep the arrangement from drooping, use several floral water picks to feed the blooms.

Pleasing Pedestal

A birch log makes an interesting pedestal for a harvest platter. Place a shiny gold plate atop a woven charger to hold the natural bounty.

Candlelight Trio

One candle's nice, but three are even better. Group together complementary candles that vary in height but coordinate in color. Add naturals, such as pinecones and leaves, to complete the lovely display. Keep anything flammable away from lit candles.

Merry Go Round

Talk about easy! Center a pillar candle on a round place mat and surround it with textural pinecones. If the cones tend to roll, use candle putty to hold them in place. A ribbon bow, tied around the candle, adds the perfect ta-da.

Juggling Act

Decorative spheres can be changed to reflect the season. These spheres, in natural tones, are the perfect autumn fit. Display them on wooden candleholders, using candle putty to keep them from rolling off. Arrange the pieces on a woven mat to help ground the collection.

Nature's Gifts

Gather pinecones from the yard to warm your home now through winter.

Lovely Branches

Capture the season's landscape with reaching twigs. Stand the branches in a glass vase and hang small pinecones from them. To support branches, tuck them among glass baubles and pinecones. Insert delicate spruce or fir shoots in the baubles. As the season transitions into winter, refresh greenery and add snowflake ornaments as shown here.

Fireplace Garland

Hang a pinecone garland along the mantel. To make it, cinch wire around the stem end of each cone running from one to the next and use thumbtacks to attach the strand where desired.

Woodland Mantel

Give your fireplace mantel northwoods charm with pinecones in painted pots and dwarf arborvitae mulched with spruce cones. Finish the scene with additional cones and juniper sprigs.

Forest in Miniature

Pinecone trees on a hearth soak up the fire's glow. Start with a decorative wire frame as shown, below. Working from the top of the frame, wedge dampened white pinecones (moisture causes them to partially close) into the frame. Secure them with dabs of hot glue. As the cones dry, they'll open fully and interlock. Stand the pinecone tree in a planter filled with gravel for support.

Gather Together

A basket wrapped in birch bark makes a lovely container to showcase a grouping of naturals, such as leaves, pinecones, twigs, greenery, berries, and cinnamon sticks. The casual display is appealing without overworking the arrangement, plus the contents can double as fire starters.

Fire Starters

Those with wood-burning fireplaces will love these fire helpers. Nest pinecones and small candles in a cardboard container filled with dried snippets of greenery and leaves. Using caution, light the wicks to set the fire starters into action.

Pumpkin Seed Place Cards

In a matter of minutes you can make place cards for all who gather around your Thanksgiving table. Start with a folded piece of cardstock and embellish with a few pumpkin seeds and a snippet of natural-tone fiber.

Humble Feast

Blanket the table with natural jute tones, setting the tone of simpler times. Drape woven place mats over the table edge to soften the look.

Pilgrim Party

Pay tribute to the Pilgrims and Indians who shared that very first Thanksgiving feast with decorations reminiscent of colonial times.

Brent

Pilgrim Hat Favor

Grace each place setting with a shabby-chic Pilgrim hat serving piece. Brush black crafts paint on a terra-cotta planter and drainage dish, allowing some of the terra-cotta color to show through; let dry. Cut a black belt to fit around the pot, hot-gluing it in place. Flip over the drainage dish and place a sweet treat on top, lining it first with food-safe paper.

Take-Home Treats

Create clever containers to hold a handful of treats for Thanksgiving guests to take home. Wrap a container, such as a frosting tub, with burlap webbing. Trim with beaded elastic string, braid, and feathers. Place snack mix, candy, or cookies in plastic treat bags and tie with suede lacing.

Quick Coasters

Squares of brightly colored woven fabric or Indian blanket make soft cushions for glassware. Tuck in quills from a couple feathers to add smart detail.

Beaded Bands

Indian corn is a natural winner with its variegated coat of kernels. Enhance its beauty with pairs of beaded bands strung on elastic thread.

Thankful Greetings

Create timely greeting cards to tell friends and family members you are thankful for them. Fold a piece of cardstock to make the desired-size card. Use double-sided tape to affix woven ribbon and braid to the card front. For a focal point, hot-glue a beaded length of suede cording to the weaving.

Pumpkin O' Plenty

Keep it natural with a hollowed-out pumpkin holding the centerpiece flowers. To make the holder, cut the top off a large pumpkin and scoop out the insides. Drill evenly spaced holes 1 inch down from top edge. Make large blanket stitches around the edge with suede lacing. Place a potted mum and tie it with a wide-braid bow. In keeping with the theme, hot-glue feathers to the end of two skewers. Wrap braid around each skewer, hot-gluing to secure. Thread beads on a length of suede lacing, knot the ends, and tie around each skewer.

Dotted Bliss

Become a master of dot painting in no time with these simple-to-do painting techniques.

Color-Laden Planter

Add a little artistic flair to a plain planter. Choose one with engraved markings to make painting a breeze. Paint in sections of the planter as desired and detail with dots marching around the rim and down the sides.

Gorgeous Gourds

Gourds are available in a plethora of interesting shapes. Enhance these natural beauties with easy-to-paint motifs and curlique wire. Coat a dried gourd with copper crafts paint; let dry. Dot the surface, using the photo as a guide. When dry, wrap coordinating wires around the stem and wrap each around a round pencil or dowel to finish.

Polka-Dot Plaque

Welcome in the season with a sign touting the colors of fall. You can layer premade wood plaques or cut your own (see pattern on page 155). Paint background colors of the wood pieces as desired using crafts paint. The dot pattern may change depending on the shape of the plaque. To make larger dots, dip a pencil eraser in paint and dot on the surface. To achieve the symmetrical look as in the photo, start in corners or in the center and make equal dots on both sides as shown. When dry, layer smaller dots using skewers, dowels, paintbrush handles, or toothpicks. Paint "Welcome Fall" on the front . Top-coat with clear polyurethane. To stand up the plaque, drill a hole in the back bottom to fit a 2-inch-long piece of ¼-inch dowel.

Finial Fun

This mini masterpiece adds a touch of autumn fun to any small space. You can use a precut wood pumpkin or cut your own using the pattern on page 154. Base-coat and dot the finial and pumpkin, using the photo for ideas. When dry, drill small holes into the bottom of the pumpkin and two into the top of the finial. Insert curled sturdy wire into the holes on the finial, hot-gluing to secure. Add the pumpkin onto the top of one wire and a bead on the other. Tiny foam, wood, or paper leaves complete the design.

Very Cute Votive Holder

Double the fun of a decorative votive holder by adding a wooden base underneath. Paint and dot a wood square that's slightly larger than the votive holder. When dry, hot-glue the votive holder atop the decorated wood square.

Meaningful Message

This whimsical little piece shares a good everyday reminder. To make it, use a precut heart or cut one using the pattern on page 154. Base-coat the heart and a wood rectangle on which to rest it. Paint "Enjoy Life" in the lower left-hand corner of the rectangle and paint dot designs around the message and on the heart as shown.

In-A-Twinkling

fall favors

No-Sew Cone

Decked out with natural burlap and buttons, this clever holder uses hot glue instead of stitches to hold things in place. Cut a piece of burlap to wrap around a cardboard cone, fraying the exposed edge. Glue burlap to cone and buttons aligned with the frayed edge. Line cone with art paper, tearing short notches into the edge.

Bow Tie

Seal up a goodie bag with a hint of autumn. Make pinecone "tassel" ties by twisting mini screw eyes into the bottom of two pinecones. Thread ends of a long cord length into the screw eyes and knot them to secure.

Goodie Basket

Personalize a miniature basket with a message of Thanksgiving. Hot-glue typewriter key replicas or alphabet beads onto the basket lip. Line with a piece of fabric and tie a ribbon bow to the handle. To help the basket sit upright, hot-glue a large metal washer to the bottom.

Pinecone Stars

Join the bottom tips of five similar-size pinecones to create a mini star. Nestle a wrapped candy in the center for a charming autumn favor.

Seasonal Symbol

Cushion a tasty sweet with a leaf shape cut from pretty scrapbook paper. Use the patterns on page 154, create your own shapes, or trace the real things, including the veins if desired. To add dimension, fold the leaf in half lengthwise, creating a center vein.

trims

Craft festive decorations to make your living space merry and bright.

Deer Delight

Encircle the season's favorite deer or other figurine with a fresh evergreen wreath dotted with pinecones. Secure the figurine in place with wire, allowing it to overlap a generous ribbon bow. Fill in the arrangement with small complementary ornaments.

First Impressions

Set the tone for wondrous holiday memories with a glorious wreath decking the door.

Initial Appeal

Quick to make, yet totally classy, this 5-minute wreath trims the front door in style. Large letters are available in a variety of materials in gift and crafts shops. Choose the initial for your last name and secure it to the wreath with wide holiday ribbon. Tie a large bow with the same ribbon, wiring it to the top.

Santa Style

Vintage or new, a St. Nick figurine greets holiday guests with playful flair. To add to the whimsy, wire an array of ornaments to one side of the jolly fellow, selecting those that match his style.

Light the Way

Create a rustic look by hanging a lantern in the wreath's center. Tie a plaid ribbon bow to the lantern handle, allowing the ribbon ends to cascade down the sides of the wreath. Use a battery-operated candle to add a gentle glow.

Great Skates

Ice skates, laced with pretty ribbon, are a timely focal point for this wintry wreath. Wire the skates in place and hot-glue a large jingle bell on each toe. Decorate the wreath with snowflake ornaments wired in place. A ribbon completes the look.

Seasonal Splendor

Turn to traditional red and green as inspiration for your next wreath. Fruits, pinecones, greenery, and ornaments are easily skewered to a large foam wreath form. Use the photo to inspire an eye-catching composition and top with a generous plaid bow.

Christmas Cheer

Let tradition ring throughout your home with striking decorations in red and white.

Christmas Cornucopia

Spreading holiday cheer is child's play with this festive cone basket. Make a handful to display around the house or just one filled with candy for a surprisingly sweet gift.

WHAT YOU NEED

Red-and-white patterned paper
Hot-glue gun and glue sticks
2 yards white crepe paper
½ yard ¾-inch-wide red velvet ribbon
½ yard ¾-inch-wide ivory velvet ribbon
½ yard 1-inch-wide red silk ribbon
Clear rhinestone
Flower appliqué
½ yard gold tinsel garland

WHAT YOU DO

1. Cut triangle shape from red-and-white patterned paper. Roll the shape into a cone; secure it with hot glue.
2. Cut a length of white crepe paper long enough to go around the top of the cone twice; machine-sew a line of basting stitches down the center. Gather the paper to fit around the top of the cone; hot-glue it in place.
3. Wrap red velvet ribbon around the center of the crepe paper, covering the stitches; glue the ends together in the center front. Referring to the photo, glue two pieces of ivory ribbon at the center front. Tie and adhere a red silk ribbon bow to the center front. Glue the rhinestone to the flower applique; glue the applique to the bow.
4. Cut a length of coordinating garland for the handle. Glue the ends of one length on opposite edges inside the cone. Tie the red silk ribbon into a bow on one side of the silver handle. Hot-glue a small amount of matching garland to the tip of the cone.

Warm Hearts

There's a bit of Christmas magic in these reverse-applique treasures. Though they look complicated, the technique is simple using wool felt and sharp scissors.

WHAT YOU NEED

Tracing paper
3 5×7-inch pieces of red felt
3 5×7-inch pieces of white felt
Dressmaker's tracing paper; pins
Red and white sewing thread
Sharp embroidery scissors that cut to a point
Pinking shears
9-inch lengths of red and white braid

WHAT YOU DO

1. Trace the applique pattern on page 155 onto tracing paper. Center the pattern on one piece of red felt and transfer the black pattern lines using dressmaker's tracing paper.
2. Center the red felt, pattern side up, on the white felt; pin the pieces together. Thread sewing machine with white thread and set the stitch length to 16 stitches per inch. Sew through both layers of felt on the transferred pattern lines. Begin sewing at the center of the design and work toward the edges, completing the large outside heart last. Pull all the thread to the red felt side; knot and trim.
3. Turn the stitched piece over to work from the white-felt side. Referring to the photograph, use embroidery scissors to carefully cut away the white felt approximately ¹⁄₁₆ inch beyond the stitching lines. At the bottom of the heart, cut three extended teardrops in the diamond shape. Use the pinking shears to trim away the white felt ¼ inch beyond the stitching lines of the large heart.
4. Center the stitched piece, right side up, on the second piece of red felt; pin together. Thread your sewing machine with red thread. Sew just beyond the pinked edges of the large white heart shape. Use the pinking shears to trim away the red felt layers approximately ¼ inch beyond the pinked white felt edge.
5. For a hanging loop, fold the 9-inch length of braid in half. Sew the braid ends to the back of the ornament at the top center.

Shrink Art Savvy

Ornaments that start at your computer finish as masterworks of shrink art. You choose the black-and-white images, adjust them for color, and print them onto shrink film. Silver foil, stamped greetings, and beads enhance the visual charm.

WHAT YOU NEED

Copyright-free floral clip art
Photo-editing computer software
Grafix shrink film sheets: Inkjet Opaque
Pencil and ruler
Permanent black ink pad
Clear acrylic stamps: assorted holiday greetings
Standard hole punch
Toaster oven or conventional oven
¼-inch-wide foil tape
Red and white glass beads
2 to 3 silver metal head pins for each ornament
Round-nose and chain-nose pliers
Flush cutters
Large silver metal jump rings
Silver metal connectors
½-inch-wide sheer white ribbons
Sterling silver jewelry wire
Wooden dowel
Terry cloth hand towel
Mallet

WHAT YOU DO

1. Select a black-and-white holiday floral digital image to print onto the shrink film. Import the image into a photo-editing software program and change the color by adjusting the hue saturation. The color will intensify when shrunk, so the lighter the clip art color, the better.
2. Follow the manufacturer's instructions to print the image directly onto the shrink film.
3. Use a pencil and ruler to draw a rectangle around a selected part of the plastic image, keeping in mind it will shrink to 30 percent of its original size; cut out the rectangle.
4. Ink your stamp and press it directly onto the rectangle.
5. Punch a hole in the center top of the rectangle. Shrink the ornament in a toaster oven or conventional oven following the manufacturer's instructions.
6. Cover the edges of the rectangle with foil tape. Burnish to remove any air bubbles.
7. String a glass bead onto each head pin. Shape each head pin into a loop with the round-nose pliers and trim the excess wire with the flush cutters. Use the chain-nose pliers to open the jump ring, then loop it through the punched hole. String the beaded head pins and connector onto the jump ring before firmly closing it.
8. Loop a 7-inch length of ribbon through the center of the connector or add another jump ring to the connector and loop ribbon through the last jump ring; knot ribbon ends together.
9. To make a metal hook, use the wire cutters and cut a 3¾-inch piece of sterling-silver wire. Using the round-nose pliers, form a small loop at one end of the wire. Form the large curve of the hook using the dowel to assist with shaping.
10. Turn the hook with the straight end up. Using the chain-nose pliers, grab the wire at the base of the straight portion of the hook. Bend the straight wire over the edge of the pliers at a 90-degree angle so the wire (when turned hook-side up) resembles the number 2.
11. Trim the wire ⅜ inch from the bend. Using round-nose pliers, create a loop in the end of the wire that will fit the ornament. Finish shaping hook as shown.
12. Fold the terry cloth hand towel into quarters. Set bench block on folded towel and place hook on the bench block. Use the mallet to pound and harden the hook.
13. With the chain-nose pliers in one hand and the flat-nose pliers in the other, open the bottom loop. Thread the open loop onto the loop of the ornament; close the loop.

Wonderland Pines

Serve up a snowy centerpiece for small or large gatherings. Cut from cardstock, each flat design comes alive as a dimensional pine. Watch them sparkle as they meander on a path of red fabric and glowing votives.

WHAT YOU NEED

Tracing paper
White cardstock
Crafts knife
Star punch (optional)
Straight pin
Crafts glue

WHAT YOU DO

1. Trace tree pattern on page 155 onto tracing paper. Tape pattern to a sunny window or a light box. Tape cardstock over pattern. Using a pencil, lightly draw the pattern onto the cardstock.
2. Using the crafts knife or the star punch, cut out stars and the two slots on the base.
3. Using the crafts knife, cut the lines for the two small inner trees. Then cut the lines for the two middle trees. When all of the inner lines are cut, cut around the entire shape.
4. Lightly score the broken lines. Mark ends of the five dotted lines with a pinhole. Turn piece over and lightly score the five lines.
5. Gently fold each oval base toward the tree along the seven scored broken lines. Note: This will force the tops of the trees to fold on the scored broken and dotted lines. Fold the piece in half at the center (top) star.
6. Dab glue between the top stars and press them together.
7. Insert the tabs into the slots at the base and secure with glue.

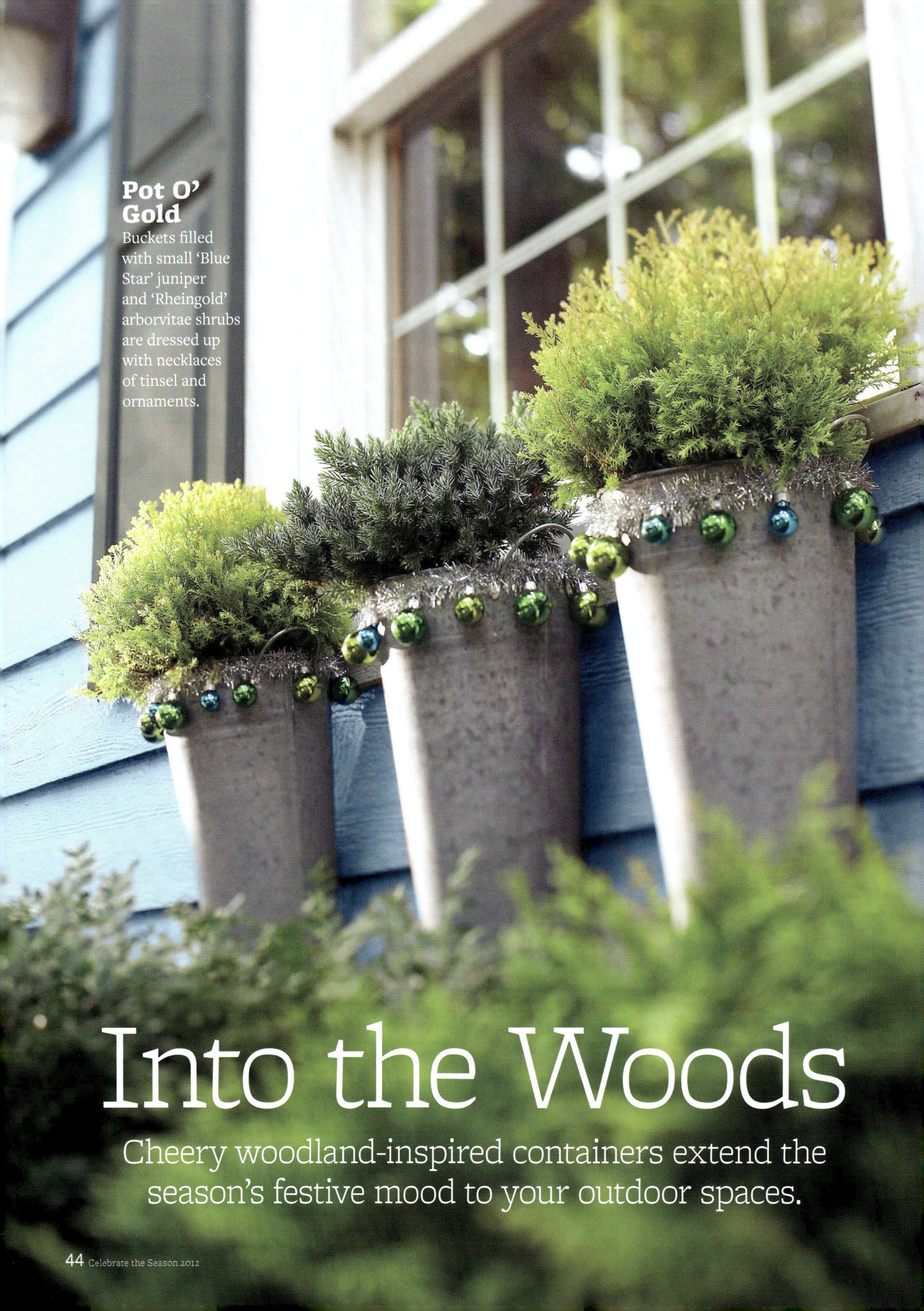

Into the Woods

Cheery woodland-inspired containers extend the season's festive mood to your outdoor spaces.

Pot O' Gold
Buckets filled with small 'Blue Star' juniper and 'Rheingold' arborvitae shrubs are dressed up with necklaces of tinsel and ornaments.

Coniferous Confection

Gather snips of evergreens and tuck them into a basket with small Hinoki false cypress. Accent with the vivid hues of Christmas ornaments.

Pinecones All Around

A super-size cone from a sugar pine, sitting atop a bed of moss and spruce sprigs, adds star power to this grouping. The design complements a potted compact 'Blue Star' juniper.

Rising Above

White twigs rise from a mound of juniper, making a small container stand tall. Snowy-white Mitsumata branches lend a striking profile and contrast with the red pot. Or go out on your own limb with redtwig dogwood, birch, or spray-painted twigs.

Simple Beauty

A store-bought boxwood ball tops this arrangement of blue spruce twigs, offering a fresh alternative to the usual upright designs.

Tiny Tannenbaums

A wrought-iron planter holder features spiral dwarf Alberta spruce and 'Rheingold' arborvitae, enhanced wth freshly cut cedar and pine boughs.

Have a Ball

Winterworthy composite planters are perfect for birch bark tubes holding 'Baby Blue' Sawara cypress and 'Mops' golden cypress. To vary the shapes, add moss and glass spheres.

Branch Out

A few snips from an evergreen tree or shrub are enough to complete an eye-catching arrangement. The pots provide most of the green in this rustic duo of pinecones and birch branches. String lights cast soft uplighting.

Nutcracker Sweet

Welcome a fine group of characters to join in the Christmas festivities. These regal fellows are sure to be conversation starters.

Upstanding Centerpiece

Fill the center of the table with a grouping of colorful nutcrackers, placing the tallest in the center. Pick up on their colors to accessorize the rest of the table. A few ornaments, snippets of greenery, and candy canes enhance the festive mood.

Nutcracker Stocking

Ready for a visit from St. Nick, this dapper soldier sports a uniform decked out with intricate detail.

WHAT YOU NEED

¾ yard 36-inch-wide wool felt for stocking front/back
¾ yard 45-inch-wide fabric for lining
Wool over-dyed fabrics for appliqué: 22×10-inch piece red herringbone for cuff; 20×3-inch piece green for cuff band; 10×8-inch piece cream for face; 10×8-inch piece black for hair, mustache, eye brows, and mouth; scrap caramel for cheeks and nose; scrap dark blue for eyes; 15×12-inch piece green herringbone for jacket; 8×4-inch piece brown for jacket epaulet; and 4×7-inch piece red for jacket front trim
Lightweight black wool fabric scrap for trim on jacket and white for eyes
5-inch square black ultra suede for star
Matching threads
⅝ yard of 1-inch-wide flat trim for cuff band
½ yard of tiny gold cord for jacket trim
8 tiny jingle bells
¼ yard of 1-inch-wide gold fringe and ¼ yard of ⅜-inch-wide flat gold trim for epaulet
6 inches of flat gold braid for hanging loop
#5 white perle cotton for eyes
Embellishment trim for star
Fusible transweb paper

Note: Seams are stitched right sides facing with ½-inch seam unless otherwise indicated. The face and jacket are constructed separately and then stitched to the stocking front.

WHAT YOU DO

1. Trace all appliqué pattern pieces from page 158 onto fusible transweb paper according to the manufacturer. Fuse each transweb pattern piece to the wrong side of corresponding fabrics. Cut out and fuse to background fabric according to pattern.

2. Machine appliqué (a close zigzag stitch) the fabric pieces with matching thread. Using photo as a guide, stitch gold fringe and trim for epaulet. Stitch gold cord to jacket front. Stitch on jingle bells. Embroider detail for eyes with perle cotton.

3. Stitch stocking front to back, leaving top edge open. Clip seams and turn to right side. Stitch lining front to back, leaving top edge open and an opening for turning. Clip seam.

4. For cuff, cut a 19×6-inch and ½-inch piece of fabric. For contrast band cut a 19×2-inch and ½-inch strip of contrast fabric. Stitch band to cuff along one long edge. Appliqué star trim to center of cuff fabric. Stitch short ends of cuff/band together. Cut a 19×8-inch cuff lining piece. Stitch short ends together. Stitch cuff lining to cuff around bottom edge, matching seam. Clip seam. Turn to right side; press. Baste raw edges together.

5. Slip cuff over stocking, matching raw edges, placing star appliqué at center front. Fold flat gold braid in half crosswise for hanging loop. Baste to cuff side seam.

6. Slip stocking into lining with right sides facing and matching seams. Stitch around top edge. Clip seam. Pull stocking through opening in stocking lining. Stitch opening closed. Smooth lining into stocking. Hand-tack lining to stocking at side seams. Add embellishment to star.

Grand Stands

To vary the height of the nutcrackers, use boxes wrapped in holiday papers. For extra pizzazz, trim with braid, doilies, or other trims.

Creative Crackers

Grace each guest's plate with an oversize cracker favor. For the base, use a mailing tube or clean food container (such as from chips). Wrap the tube with a double layer of tissue paper, cut 4 inches longer on both ends. Glue a piece of cardstock around the tube and trim with braid, ribbon, and mini plastic ornaments or large beads. Cinch tissue paper at one end and tie closed with ribbon. Fill favor with wrapped candies or other small gifts and close with ribbon.

Treat Cups

Fitting with the theme, mixed nuts are a welcome snack at each guest's place setting. Edge small plastic bowls with braid glued in place. Guard each bowl with a take-home nutcracker ornament to remind each guest of this special Christmas gathering for many years to come.

Pretty Palette
Choose coordinating felt colors to lend a feeling of continuity to room decor.

Felted & Fabulous

Craft keepsake holiday treasures from rich-toned textural wool felt.

Bow Dazzle

Add a little "aha" to your holiday wreath by crafting a cheery felted bow. Cut a 4×12-inch piece of felt for the loops. Felt on polka dots and hot-glue small felt beads to some of the centers. Edge with a narrow strip of contrasting felt. Cut a 3×8-inch piece of felt for the center; edge with narrow felt strips. Use the pattern on page 157 to cut two ribbon tails; edge with narrow strips. Using a needle and embroidery floss, stitch the ends of the loop piece together. Wrap the center piece around the loop; stitch to secure. Sew the tails to the bow back.

Felt Flakes

Pressed felt snowflakes fill in tree branches in a hurry. To add dimension, hot-glue felt beads in contrasting color to the centers.

Ta-Da Topper

Top the tree with a star felted in bright tones. Use the patterns on page 157 to cut the star, triangles, and center circles. Felt the yellow star to a white background and trim a narrow border. Continue adding pieces as shown, using a felting tool. Use straight stitches to secure the felt bead in the center. Sew a felt loop on the back to hold star to the tree.

Merry Mittens

Like snowflakes, none of these mittens are alike. Simple wool felt shapes or wool roving designs detail each ornament front. An embroidery floss loop hangs them on branches or ties them to package ribbon.

WHAT YOU NEED

Tracing paper
Pencil
Scissors
Felting needle tool
Felting brush
Wool felt
Wool roving
Felted balls
Embroidery floss and needle

WHAT YOU DO

1. Trace the mitten pattern on page 157; cut out. Use the pattern to cut top mitten layer from desired color of wool felt.
2. Decide the design you like, using the photo for inspiration. Cut solid shapes from wool felt or use roving to make lines.
3. Place the mitten top on the felting brush. Arrange the felt shape or roving on the mitten top as shown in Photo A. Following the manufacturer's directions, pounce the felting tool onto the felt piece or roving until well secured. Continue adding and layering pieces until design is complete.
4. Cut a piece of wide roving for the cuff, doubling if necessary to reach desired thickness. Tack the cuff to the mitten top using the felting needle tool as shown in Photo B.
5. Place the mitten top on the slightly larger mitten back; place on felting brush. Pounce the felting needle tool around the edge of the mitten top to secure the two layers together as shown in Photo C.
6. Sew one or two felted balls to the right corner of the cuff using embroidery floss and a large cross-stitch as shown in Photo D.

Snow Family

These fluffy snowmen and tree can be made in a variety of sizes depending on the foam balls chosen. For the body, cut a sliver off the bottom of the larger foam ball so the snowman sits upright. Using white wool roving and a multi-needle felting tool, wrap roving around foam ball, pouncing the tool through the roving into the ball until secure; repeat for the head. Use a toothpick to connect the two wrapped foam balls together, adding crafts glue if desired. Roll up small pieces of felt or roving to make eyes and carrot noses. To make a top hat, cut two circles for the top and a slightly larger circle for the brim piece. Felt the brim circle to the snowman's head; add the two top pieces. For the winter cap, cut a circle slightly larger than the snowman head; cut four narrow pie shapes from the opposite sides, leaving the center uncut. Stitch a felt bead in the center and attach to the head. Use roving to create the soft brim. Two circles and a narrow band create earmuffs. Felt narrow strips into scarves and tack in place. To make the tree, wrap and felt two tones of green roving around the tree; add circle ornaments and twisted red and white roving pieces to resemble candy canes. Use the diamond patterns on page 156 to craft the star.

Ring Around the Napkin

Guests will know they're in for a special meal when they pull their napkins from these festive rings. To make one, cut a 3×8 piece of red felt. Cut three ½-inch circles from white felt. Felt the circles evenly spaced along one short end of red felt. Sew a red jingle bell in the center of each white circle. Trim the long edges with a narrow piece of green felt, twisting it as it is felted. Create a design using green felt strips along the ends opposite the bells. Stitch the strip into a ring.

Who's It From?

Craft a cute character to hang out on top of a special gift. To make the owl, use the patterns on page 157. Cut the pieces from wool felt. Using the photo as a guide, felt beak, face details, and tummy shading to background. Felt a wing to each side, fold to front, and felt wing tip to hold in place. Fold over head and felt beak in place.

Cozy Throw

Jazz up a blanket with a felted scene. Use the patterns on page 156. To make ornaments and roof lights, roll up small sections of roving and felt in place. Use wisps of roving for chimney smoke and landscape background and thicker pieces for trees and bushes.

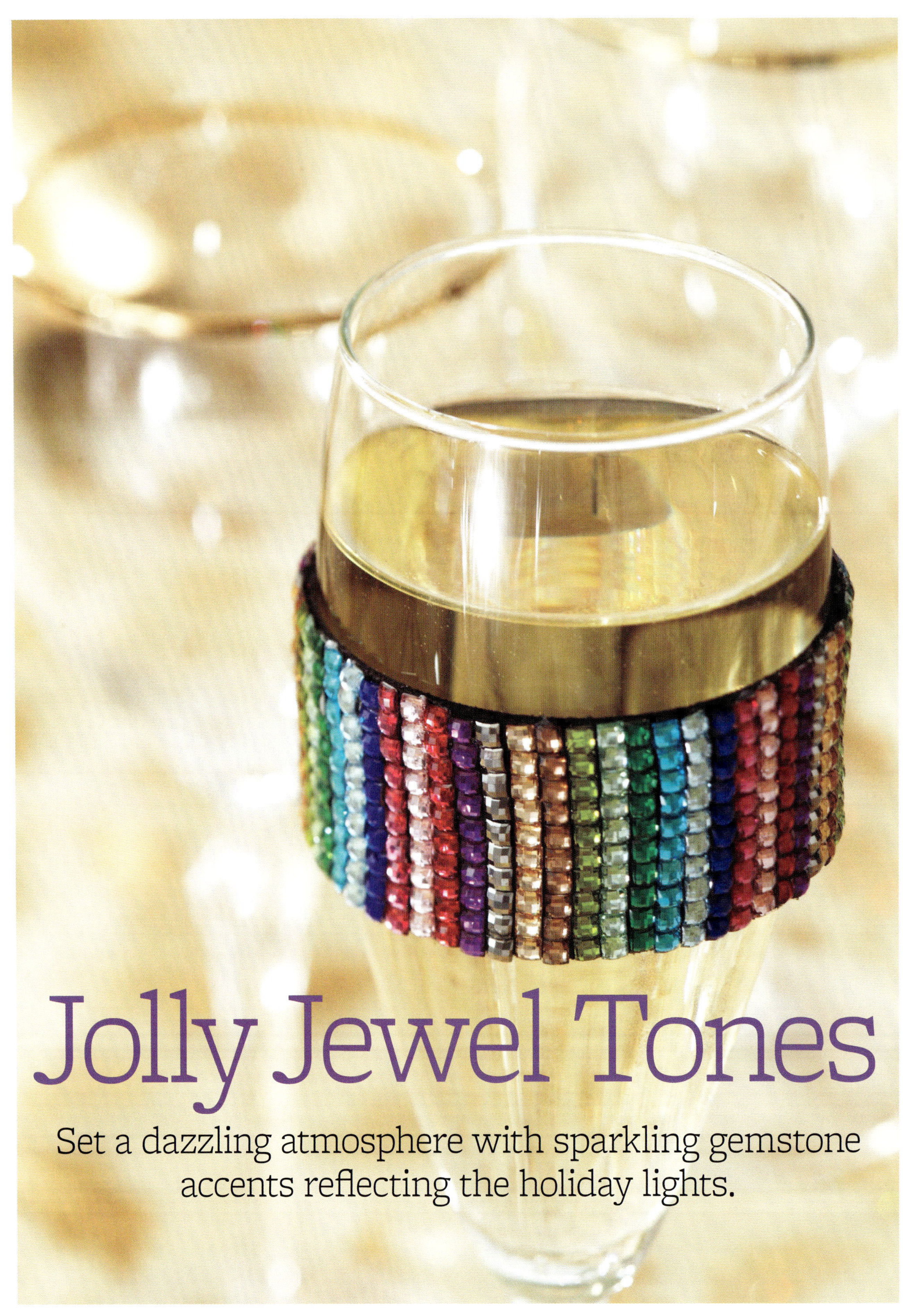

Jolly Jewel Tones

Set a dazzling atmosphere with sparkling gemstone accents reflecting the holiday lights.

Bracelet Bangles

Girlfriends will be thrilled to discover that the bright band on their glass is actually a bracelet favor. If the bangle doesn't want to stay put, a few small strips of double-sided tape will help hold it in place.

Merry Wishes

Welcome each guest to the table with an endearing holiday message. Cut out messages from old Christmas cards, mount on pretty papers, and accent the sentiment with press-on gems.

Single-Serving Surprise

Whether served that night or offered as a take-home gift, individual wine bottles are a welcome present. Slip an elastic-band ring over the bottle's neck for two gifts in one.

Elegant Candles

Dress candles for the season with a lineup of press-on gems adhered to the glass cup. Place the gems in the same color order for a unified look or vary the placement for a more casual appearance.

Beauty and the Bobble

Costume earrings, embedded with radiant stones, make gorgeous accents for plain holiday ornaments. Use wire cutters to snip off earring posts or clips. Then use a low-temp glue gun to adhere the fancy findings to ornaments.

Lost Cause

When you lose a single earring, don't throw the other out. Whether pierced or clip, use the earring to add a spectacular touch to the center of a ribbon bow adorning a holiday gift.

Unforgettable Napkin Ties

A lovely wide ribbon tied around a dinner napkin makes an easy napkin ring. Dot the knot with a gemmed pin or earring, and the ring dazzles.

Woven Wonders

Whether using ribbons or paper strips, weaving combines holiday colors into trendy trims.

Pretty Pillow

A premade pillow in a favorite wintry hue makes the perfect backdrop for a field of lovely woven ribbons.

WHAT YOU NEED

Foam core cut to pillow size
Nonwired ribbons, cut 3 inches shorter than pillow
Square premade pillow
Straight pins
Scissors
Lightweight fusible interfacing
Iron
Ribbon to edge weaving
Sewing machine
Matching thread and sewing needle

WHAT YOU DO

1. Working on top of the piece of foam core, weave the ribbons together, right sides down. Pin the ends of each ribbon piece to the foam core.
2. Cut a piece of interfacing the size of the weaving. Following the manufacturer's directions, fuse the interfacing to the back side of the woven ribbons, removing pins once center portion is secure. Trim edges straight if needed.
3. Machine-stitch ribbon along the right side of each edge of weaving to cover the cut ends. Handstitch the weaving to the pillow top.

Over and Out

Craft a gift tag that's so cute it will find its way onto the tree once the gifts are unwrapped. Weave paper strips into a small square, securing on one side with packing tape. Cut the secured woven piece into a circle and hot-glue a silver chenille stem around the edge, making a loop at the top. Cut a small rectangle from white paper and write gift recipient's name on it. Back with colored paper and trim a narrow border. Hot-glue to the top of the tag.

Vintage Celebration

Thanks to vintage-looking materials, these handcrafted decorations recall Christmases of long ago.

Gift-Box Decor

There's no peeking into these packages. Using 3½-inch wooden cubes, cut six paper squares slightly smaller than sides. Glue squares on cube sides, adding trims as desired. Draw faux sewing lines along edges if desired. Ink cube edges with brown. Apply a coat of varnish; let dry. Tie each package with a ribbon bow.

Starlight Delight

Chipboard stars—one covered in sheet music and inked, the other ablaze with German glass glitter—frame a vintage-look Santa face with Victorian-style charm. The starry design is displayed on an antique silver frog.

WHAT YOU NEED

Large and small chipboard stars
Old sheet music
Crafts glue
Red raised-felt dye ink pad
Ink blending tool
Vintage-style Santa face paper cutout
Dimensional adhesive dots
Ecru print and solid scrapbook paper
Double-sided tape
Silver ultrafine German glass glitter
Antique silver frog (optional)
Wire hanging hook (optional)

WHAT YOU DO

1. Using the small chipboard star as a template, trace star onto old sheet music. Cut out shape and glue to glossy white side of small chipboard star; let dry. Using an ink blending tool and starting at the edges, spread ink onto sheet-music-covered star; blend ink into the center; let dry. Secure Santa face cutout to center of star using two adhesive dots.

2. From ecru print scrapbook paper, cut a ½×3½-inch strip. Cut an inverted V into each end of strip. Referring to photo, accordion-fold ends to create banner. Using a computer and desired font, print Merry Christmas to measure ¾ inch long on ecru paper; cut out sentiment and glue to center front of banner. Glue banner across Santa beard.

3. Cover large chipboard star with double-sided adhesive tape; trim excess tape. Adhere small star to center of large star with two adhesive dots. Sprinkle ultrafine German glass glitter over large star, shaking off excess.

4. Perch finished star in frog or punch a hole in the top of the star and add a wire hanging hook.

Santa Treasure

With crepe paper ruffles, music print paper, and vintage-looking ephemera, this dolled-up container hits just the right note as a gift box for a special trinket or a sweet decoration to place on a nightstand.

WHAT YOU NEED

3×2½-inch round papier-mâché box
White and red acrylic paint
Christmas music paper
Decoupage medium, such as Mod Podge
White cardstock
Christmas images; Santa and greeting
Brush-on gloss glaze; white and red glitter
Hot-glue gun and glue sticks
Thick crafts glue; red crepe paper

WHAT YOU DO

1. Paint the box white and the lid red. Cut a piece of music paper to fit around the box and adhere it with decoupage medium.
2. Photocopy the Christmas images onto cardstock. Use the decoupage medium to adhere the images to the back of the music paper; let dry. Cut out the images, leaving a ½-inch-wide margin along the bottom of each. Fold the strips into tabs for gluing.
3. Apply the glaze to both images; let dry. Apply the glaze to other areas as desired and sprinkle with white glitter; let dry.
4. Hot-glue the images to the top of the lid. Apply crafts glue to the outside of the lid and sprinkle with red glitter. Cut and stack two 12-inch lengths of crepe paper; gather into a ruffled circle. Place a drop of glue in the center of the circle and sprinkle with red glitter. Hot-glue the circle to the lid.
5. For ruffle, cut two 28-inch lengths of crepe paper. Stack strips and make a running stitch ¼ inch from edge of one long side. Pull thread to gather into a circle; tie off thread. Hot-glue ruffle to bottom of box.

Christmas Tree Concerto

Composed of seasonal sheet music, this music-lover's tree hits a high note as a tabletop centerpiece or a mantel display. Underneath, a 9-inch foam cone makes pinning the paper loops in place a cinch.

WHAT YOU NEED

Vintage sheet music
Patterned paper
Straight pins
Plastic foam cone, 9 inches tall with a 4-inch base
Hot-glue gun and glue sticks
5 inches of ¼-inch-wide ecru lace trim
1-inch-diameter rust-finish jingle bell

WHAT YOU DO

1. From sheet music and patterned paper (see Photo A), cut ½ × 4-inch strips (about 150 from sheet music and about 40 from patterned paper). Bend a sheet-music strip in half to make a loop without folding as shown in Photo B. Pin ends of loop to bottom of cone with loop toward work surface as in Photo C. Continue to fold and pin loops around bottom of cone, adding a few patterned-paper loops as accents.

2. Pin another row of loops to cone, placing new loops between first-row loops and low enough so they cover pins in first row. Continue covering cone with rows of loops, working toward top of cone. For the top row, fold the cut ends of the loops flat over the top of the cone and pin them in place.

3. Pin lace trim around top of cone; cut excess trim. Hot-glue jingle bell to top of cone as shown in Photo D.

A

B

C

D

Casual Style

Holiday decor need not tout traditional hues. Choose colors and patterns that complement your decorating to enhance your everyday style.

By the Chimney With Care

Decorator fabrics look tres chic transformed into stockings ready to be filled with holiday surprises.

WHAT YOU NEED

Pencil
Tracing paper
Scissors
Decorator fabric
Straight pins
1¼-inch button forms, optional
Piping
Matching thread
Matching embroidery floss
Sewing machine

WHAT YOU DO

1. Trace and enlarge the pattern on page 155; cut out Use the pattern pieces to cut a stocking front and back, and a cuff piece if desired.

2. For the cuffed stocking, align a piece of piping along the bottom edge of cuff, raw edges even; machine-stitch in place. Turn raw edges under; topstitch. Pin cuff piece on stocking front, aligning tops.

3. For the piped stocking, pin piping to stocking front, using the placement line on pattern as a guide. Stitch piping in place using matching thread.

4. Pin stocking front to back, right sides facing. Stitch using a ½-inch seam. Clip seams; turn right side out.

5. Fold top edge under ¼ inch twice; topstitch.

6. To add buttons, cover a button form following the manufacturer's directions. Hot-glue piping around the edge. Sew three covered buttons to the right of the piping as shown.

7. To make a bow, cut a 6-inch square of fabric; fray the edges. Accordion-fold the fabric; tie with floss in center. Trim excess fabric off a short piece of piping; hot-glue around bow center. Stitch a hanging loop from embroidery floss on the upper right-hand corner of stocking.

Package Pizzazz

Keep the color scheme intact, wrapping gifts in papers that blend with the decor. Jingle bells and mini ornaments complete the look.

Sitting Pretty

Dress the table in keeping with your home's colors, even if it's an unexpected color combination, such as olive and pink. To unite the look, choose gold or silver as a companion color and have fun pulling the colors into play through ornaments, dishes, fabrics, and candles.

Merry Votives

Votive candles are readily available in a rainbow of hues. Choose those that go with the color palette to bring light to the table. Embellish the holders with a ring of ribbon and snippets from an artificial floral pick hot-glued to the glass.

Cheerful Charger

Personalize plastic plate chargers for the season by adding pleated ornamentation. Accordion-fold a 4-inch square of fabric and secure in the center with a chenille stem. Drill a pair of holes through the charger, feed through the chenille stems ends, and twist to secure.

Sweet Sentiments

Adorn each guest's glass with a festive paper charm. Use a small piece of paper with a meaningful word on it; edge with chenille stem. Punch a hole at the top and tie it to the glass stem with ribbon.

O Christmas Tree

With endless scrapbook paper choices, crafting this tree in your favorite tones is a breeze. Use the patterns on page 157 to cut shapes. Use a glue stick to adhere pieces to background and hot-glue to edge the tree, trunk, and snow with chenille stems. Cover a papier-mâché star with diamond-shape pieces cut to fit each point. Insert tree with background into a frame. Hot-glue star in place for the crowning glory.

Go Green

A candle makes a spectacular focal point for a holiday centerpiece. Surround it with sprigs of evergreen to cushion a sea of pinecones and ornaments.

Under Wraps

Can't find that just-right wrapping paper? Get rave reviews using decorative wallpaper, art paper, and shelving liner. Top the gifts with coordinating ribbons and plastic ornaments for unforgettable looks.

Grand Banister

Add a touch of playfulness to banister greenery with the addition of small boxes wrapped with holiday flair. Fill in the display with plastic ornaments, tied on with pretty bows.

Festive Fruit

Fresh or crafted, fruit conveys your best holiday wishes.

Sentimental Pears

If words sometimes fail you, use your artistic ways to share your message. This luscious arrangement is filled with loving thoughts handwritten on the pear sculptures. Made from air-dry clay and topped with a muslin leaf, each fruit is a beauty of natural proportions and hues.

WHAT YOU NEED

Aluminum foil
8-ounce package air-dry clay
Nylon kitchen sponge
Large flat paintbrush
Fine-grit sandpaper
Yellow, gold, red, light green, and antique gold acrylic paints
Dark brown antiquing glaze
Paste wax
Black oil-based opaque paint pen
4×6-inch muslin piece
Hot-glue gun and glue sticks

1. Shape foil into a pear shape, pressing it against worktable to make a tight shape. Use a spoon handle to indent top for leaf placement.
2. Cut a 2-inch cube of clay and pat or roll it until it is ⅛ inch thick. Wrap clay around foil pear, smoothing seams with lightly moistened fingertips. Add texture to pear with sponge. Air-dry pear overnight or bake it in a 200°F oven for 1 hour. Lightly sand surface and wipe away sanding dust.
3. Base-coat all surfaces with yellow paint; let dry. Crosshatch-stroke one-third of pear from top to bottom using gold paint. With dry brush and antique gold, paint the edges of the crosshatch area using a damp paper towel to blend colors. Paint center of gold area from top to bottom with red.
4. Apply antiquing glaze over surface of pear. Wait 5 minutes, then wipe clean with a slightly damp paper towel. Let dry for 30 minutes. Rub pear with paste wax. Wait 10 minutes; gently wipe off excess. Let dry for 1 hour.
5. Use paint pen to add sentiment, such as "My love for you is sweet and grows with every new season," around pear. If you make a mistake, allow ink to dry for 2 minutes, then rub paste wax over the error to erase the ink. Let dry for 1 hour before continuing.
6. From muslin, cut a leaf shape to fit pear top. Paint both sides of leaf light green. When dry, fray the edges. Hot-glue leaf to top of pear.

Seasonal Sprigs

Fresh greenery through the house adds ambience to every holiday gathering.

Let It Snow

Turn inexpensive glass cylinders into little winter wonderlands. Place one cylinder inside a larger one, sprinkle fake snow between the two, and add a sprig of cedar. Pop a votive or pillar candle into the inner cylinder.

Mini Wreath

Don't leave your kitchen out of the decorating fun. Snip a few sprigs from your holiday tree or yard, add some berries, and tie into a small ring with florist wire.

Season's Eatings

This casual place setting shows simple can be beautiful. Its personality started with a cleverly folded "pocket" napkin. Artfully arrange the silverware, outline with grapevine twigs, and tuck in a wisp of juniper to make the place setting come alive.

Bouquets to Go

To make fragrant chair-back decorations, scour the garden and grocery store for fresh herbs. Bundle bay leaf, thyme, rosemary, and marjoram with twine, leaving tails to tie around the chair. The bouquets can be made several days in advance, then refrigerated.

Come On In

Woven jute ribbon makes a textural background for a quaint door trim. Use adhesive letters to add a vertical message and top the trim with fresh greenery and pinecones wired to the top.

Greetings of the Season

A pretty table makes a celebration memorable. For each guest's napkin ring, write a personal message on a holiday coaster, punch a hole in the top, and tie with jingle bells. Tuck in a snippet of greenery.

Organic Art

Switch out art in existing frames or buy inexpensive shadow boxes and/or frames with mats. Cut new backgrounds out of burlap or colored paper, then use hot glue to mount twigs or varied evergreen sprigs for art naturally themed to the season.

Top That

Here's a gift that's almost too pretty to open. Snug a greenery twig to a wrapped package with a band of ribbon. Wire small ornaments to the sprouts to resemble a miniature Christmas tree.

In Stitches

Simple stitches warm holiday accents with homespun style.

Check It Out

Checked paper makes cross-stitching as easy as paint-by-number. Lay the paper flat on a piece of plastic foam. Use a needle to poke holes in the corners of the paper where stitches are desired. Working carefully so the paper doesn't wrinkle, use embroidery floss or decorative narrow ribbon to make cross-stitches on the paper using the illustration on page 154 as a guide.

Sock Favor

A perfect little gift, this paper sock is just the right size to hold a candy cane or two. Use the pattern on page 156 to cut out two stocking shapes. Place them atop each other on a sheet of plastic foam and poke holes ¼ inch apart and ¼ inch in from edge. Use embroidery floss to edge the stocking with blanket stitches. Hot-glue a button and pom-pom to the right-hand corner. Twist on a chenille stem, shaping the ends into curliques.

Beribboned Tag

A paper tag takes on Christmas charm with the addition of gingham ribbon and a dimensional stitched letter emblem. Stitch contrasting Xs on the ribbon and glue it around the tag. Use dabs of hot glue to adhere the monogram.

Wood Trims

Wooden shapes, dabbed, brushed, and sprayed with paint, make clever keepsake ornaments.

Sparkling Snowflakes

A big imagination and a lot of wooden pieces get snowflakes underway. Use precut shapes, beads, pegs, golf tees, and plugs. Start with a larger flat piece on which to hot-glue the spokes. Add pieces until the desired look is achieved. Spray-paint silver; sprinkle with silver glitter while wet.

Old-Fashioned Fun

Create vintage-looking ornaments using wooden miniature trees, wagon wheels, and finials. Hot-glue pieces together; paint sections with acrylic paint. When dry, edge shapes with a light dusting of white paint. Spray with clear sealer. When dry, twist a tiny screw eye in one end and thread with ribbon.

Frosted Frosty

Add fun to tree branches with rustic characters. To create one, hot-glue a wooden bead to a ball. Drill a tiny hole in each side of ball for toothpick arms; hot-glue in place. For hat, glue a checker and two wood wheels to top of head. Paint ornament black; let dry. Use a stencil brush to dot white onto trim as shown; sprinkle with glitter. Dot two black eyes and a copper nose. For scarf, cut a newspaper strip; glue in place. Glue a button in center and chenille stem to ends.

Dazzling Icicles

Spindles, golf tees, and end caps create pretty shapes reminiscent of icicles. Hot-glue the pieces together, paint white, and sprinkle with white or clear glitter to enhance the icy effect.

New Year's Cheer

Ring in the New Year with easy-to-do decorations that can be completed even when guests are on their way.

When the Clock Strikes

Let party headwear double as a napkin holders. Shape a cardboard tiara around the napkin and wrap chenille stem around the ends to secure. Tuck in a fresh flower for each guest to take home when the evening is over.

Party Hat Centerpiece

Integrate a floral arrangement with a Happy New Year top hat. Use a crafts knife to cut an X into the top of the hat, just large enough to fit a small circular vase. Fold the flaps down and insert the vase from the top. Pour water in the vase and add a colorful flower arrangement, jazzed up with silvery floral picks.

Who Sits Where

Recycle wine and champagne corks into classy place card holders. Use a crafts knife to cut a small slit in one side as shown. Hot-glue narrow ribbon around the cork bottom. Make a name card from scrapbook papers and slip it into the cork slit.

In-A-Twinkling

card cut-ups

Too-Cute Tags

Give holiday cards a second chance by making them into adorable package tags. Use a tag punch to create the shape and trim with chenille stem and other small trims. For professional polish, punch a hole near the top and finish with a metal eyelet.

Frame It

Many greeting cards are frameworthy and make wonderful gifts. Simply cut off the back of the card and slip it into a frame. Add a ribbon bow and grouping of small pinecones to one corner for a festive accent.

Star Ornament

Like a patchwork quilt design, five diamond sections join to create a star shape. Choose cards whose colors and themes coordinate. Use the patterns on page 154 to cut the shapes. Use a glue stick to adhere the diamonds to the star background shape. Define the edges with pieces of chenille stem hot-glued into place.

Quick Coasters

With no two alike, these clever coasters are great conversation starters. Cut out squares from greeting cards, mount on cardstock, and then laminate the layers together. Hot-glue chenille stem around the edge to complete the look.

food

Make the holidays memorable with festive foods and drinks that offer a hint of decadence. Be it a cocktail party, brunch, sit-down feast, or homemade cookies and candy, it's all meant to be shared.

APPETIZER ALBONDIGAS
Recipe on page 97

ROSEMARY BRUSCHETTA STACKS
Recipe on page 97

Throw a Party!

Add a little extra cheer and excitement to the scene with savory bites and bits of bubbly.

PECAN- AND CHERRY-TOPPED BRIE

Appetizer Albondigas

In Mexico, meatballs are most commonly found in soups, but your guests will love eating them on top of tortilla chips. Pictured on page 94.

1 egg, lightly beaten
½ cup finely chopped onion
3 tablespoons yellow cornmeal
2 tablespoons snipped fresh cilantro
1 tablespoon finely chopped chipotle peppers in adobo sauce*
¾ teaspoon dried oregano, crushed
½ teaspoon ground cumin
¼ teaspoon salt
12 ounces ground beef
12 ounces ground pork
32 tortilla chips
½ cup shredded Mexican-style four-cheese blend
Fresh salsa

1. Preheat oven to 425°F. In a large bowl combine egg, onion, cornmeal, cilantro, chipotle peppers, oregano, cumin, and salt. Add beef and pork; mix well.
2. Shape meat mixture into 32 meatballs. Place meatballs ½ inch apart in a 15×10×1-inch baking pan. Bake, uncovered, for 12 to 15 minutes or until meatballs are cooked through (160°F), checking with an instant-read thermometer.
3. Remove pan from oven. Using a spatula, place meatballs on tortilla chips on a clean baking pan. Sprinkle with cheese. Bake for 2 to 3 minutes more or until cheese melts. Transfer appetizers to a serving platter. Serve with salsa. Makes 32 meatballs.
***Test Kitchen Tip:** Canned chipotle peppers contain volatile oils that can burn your skin and eyes, so avoid direct contact with them as much as possible. When working with the chiles, wear disposable plastic or rubber gloves. If your bare hands do touch the chiles, wash your hands and nails thoroughly with soap and hot water.

Rosemary Bruschetta Stacks

Rosemary, with its penetrating aroma, wakes up the taste of the mellower ingredients in this simple appetizer. The sprigs, although full of flavor, are not meant to be eaten. Pictured on page 95.

3 tablespoons butter, softened
1 clove garlic, minced
12 ¼-inch slices baguette-style French bread
2 ¼-inch slices provolone cheese (2 ounces), each cut into 6 pieces
6 slices roma tomatoes
6 4-inch fresh rosemary sprigs
Kosher salt or salt (optional)
Freshly ground black pepper (optional)

1. Preheat oven to 425°F. Line a baking sheet with foil; set aside. In a small bowl combine butter and garlic. Lightly spread butter mixture on one side of each bread slice. Place a piece of cheese on the buttered side of each of six of the bread slices; top each with a tomato slice, another piece of cheese, and a remaining bread slice, buttered side down.
2. Pull the leaves off the bottom 2 inches of each rosemary sprig. Push a sprig into each stack to hold it together. Place stacks on the prepared baking sheet.
3. Bake about 4 minutes or until cheese is starting to melt. Serve warm. If desired, sprinkle lightly with salt and pepper. Makes 6 appetizers.

POMEGRANATE COSMO PUNCH

Pecan- and Cherry-Topped Brie

Add sparkle to an appetizer buffet by including soft buttery-Brie cheese topped with honey-sweetened fruit and nuts. Serve with with savory puff pastry squares. If you prefer Brie that is slightly melted, place the appetizer in a 350°F oven for 10 minutes.

½ of a 17.3-ounce package (1 sheet) frozen puff pastry sheets, thawed
1 egg, lightly beaten
1 tablespoon water
½ teaspoon coarse salt
½ teaspoon snipped fresh thyme
¼ teaspoon freshly ground black pepper
½ cup chopped pecans, toasted
⅓ cup snipped dried tart cherries
2 tablespoons honey
1 8-ounce round Brie cheese

1. Preheat oven to 375°F. Line a large baking sheet with parchment paper; set aside. Unfold puff pastry on a lightly floured surface. If necessary, roll pastry into a 9-inch square. Using a sharp knife or a pastry wheel, cut pastry into 1½-inch squares. Place pastry squares 1 inch apart on the prepared baking sheet.
2. In a small bowl combine egg and the water. Lightly brush egg mixture onto pastry squares. In another small bowl combine salt, thyme, and pepper. Sprinkle mixture over pastry squares.
3. Bake for 10 to 12 minutes or until pastry is puffed and golden brown. Cool slightly.
4. Meanwhile, in a small bowl combine pecans, dried cherries, and honey. Place cheese on a serving platter. Top cheese with some of the pecan mixture. Serve with warm pastry squares. Pass the remaining pecan mixture. Makes 8 servings.
Hazelnut- and Apricot-Topped Brie: Prepare as directed, except substitute chopped hazelnuts (filberts) for the pecans, snipped dried apricots for the cherries, and apricot preserves for the honey.

Pomegranate Cosmo Punch

Do you love fancy drinks but detest the work of making individual cocktails? Serve Cosmopolitans in a punch!

4 cups pomegranate juice, chilled
½ of a 12-ounce can frozen limeade concentrate, thawed (¾ cup)
4 cups lemon-lime carbonated beverage, chilled
2 cups orange vodka or vodka
⅓ cup orange liqueur
Ice cubes
Orange peel twists (optional)*

1. In a punch bowl combine pomegranate juice and concentrate. Slowly pour lemon-lime beverage down side of bowl. Add vodka and liqueur; stir gently to mix. Add ice cubes. If desired, garnish with orange peel twists. Makes 14 (6-ounce) servings.
***Test Kitchen Tip:** To make twists for a crowd, cut off ends of 1 or 2 oranges. Using a spoon, loosen flesh around the pulp and pop out the pulp. Cut the peel lengthwise; roll peel up jelly-roll style and secure with a toothpick. Cut peel into ⅛-inch slices.

SWISS OLIVE GALETTE

Swiss Olive Galette

Gruyère is an aged Swiss cheese with a nutty flavor that pairs nicely with leeks, fennel, and olives. Using refrigerated piecrust makes this rustic tart extra easy. Simply fold the pastry dough up over the filling and bake.

- ½ of a 15-ounce package rolled refrigerated unbaked piecrust (1 crust)
- 1 tablespoon olive oil
- 1 cup finely chopped leeks (white part only)
- ½ cup finely chopped fresh fennel
- ¾ cup coarsely chopped Kalamata olives
- 1 tablespoon snipped fresh thyme
- 4 ounces Gruyère cheese, shredded (1 cup)
- Snipped fresh fennel tops (optional)

1. Allow piecrust to stand at room temperature according to package directions. Preheat oven to 375°F. Line a large baking sheet with parchment paper; set aside. Roll pastry into an 11-inch circle on prepared baking sheet.
2. In a medium skillet heat olive oil over medium heat. Cook leeks and fennel in hot oil for 5 to 6 minutes or until tender but not brown. Remove from heat. Stir in olives and thyme. Cool slightly.
3. Spread mixture in the center of the pastry, leaving a 1½-inch rim uncovered on the edge. Fold uncovered pastry up over filling. Top with cheese.
4. Bake for 30 to 35 minutes or until pastry is golden. If desired, sprinkle with snipped fennel tops. Cut into wedges and serve warm. Makes 6 to 8 servings.

Crunchy Asian Party Mix

To make your own wasabi-flavor peas, place 5 cups of dried peas in a bowl. Lightly coat peas with nonstick cooking spray. Sprinkle with 2 to 3 teaspoons wasabi powder and toss to coat.

- 5 cups purchased wasabi-flavor dehydrated peas*
- 4 cups bite-size toasted rice cracker mix or rice square cereal
- 4 cups sesame sticks and/or crisp mixed vegetable sticks
- 4 cups honey-roasted peanuts or whole unsalted cashews
- 2 cups coconut chips

1. In an extra-large bowl combine wasabi-flavor peas, rice cracker mix, sesame sticks and/or crisp mixed vegetable sticks, peanuts, and coconut chips. Transfer mixture to an airtight container. Cover and store at room temperature for up to 1 week or freeze for up to 4 months. Makes 20 cups or 80 (¼-cup) servings.
***Test Kitchen Tip:** Wasabi peas can be found in Asian markets or in the Asian section of larger supermarkets.

Jamaican Jerk Shrimp with Papaya and Pineapple

Holiday guests will delight in this sunny Carribean-style appetizer. Present the colorful mixture on one or more platters. Or serve individual portions of fruit and shrimp in chilled martini glasses.

- 2 pounds frozen peeled, cooked large shrimp (with tails)
- 1 tablespoon Jamaican jerk seasoning*
- 1 tablespoon vegetable oil
- 1½ to 2 cups coarsely chopped, canned tropical fruit such as pineapple, mango, and/or papaya
- ¼ cup chopped roasted red sweet peppers
- ¼ cup sliced green onions
- 1 teaspoon finely shredded lime peel
- 2 tablespoons lime juice
- 2 cloves garlic, minced

1. Thaw shrimp. Place shrimp in a resealable plastic bag. Add jerk seasoning and oil to shrimp. Seal bag; turn to coat shrimp. Chill for 30 minutes.
2. Meanwhile, in a medium bowl combine tropical fruit, roasted peppers, sliced green onions, lime peel, lime juice, and garlic. Cover and chill until serving time.
3. To serve, gently stir together shrimp and fruit mixture. Transfer mixture to a serving platter. Makes 12 servings.
***Test Kitchen Tip:** Look for Jamaican jerk seasoning in the herb and spice section of a large supermarket. Or to make your own homemade seasoning, combine 1½ teaspoons dried thyme, ½ teaspoon ground allspice, ½ teaspoon black pepper, ⅛ teaspoon salt, ⅛ teaspoon ground cinnamon, and ⅛ teaspoon cayenne pepper.

CRUNCHY ASIAN PARTY MIX

JAMAICAN JERK SHRIMP WITH PAPAYA AND PINEAPPLE

Festive Brunch

Welcome Christmas or the New Year with delicious morning favorites. Much of the prep work on these showstoppers can be done ahead of time, which will help keep the festivities flowing smoothly.

SUGAR AND SPICE STEAMED PUDDING
Recipe on page 102

HAM-ASPARAGUS STRATA
Recipe on page 102

Sugar and Spice Steamed Pudding

Steamed pudding, basically a stovetop cake cooked in a Dutch oven over simmering water, comes out moist and tender. With spices and candied fruit it's the perfect holiday stand-in for coffee cake. Serve it at room temperature or reheated. Pictured on page 100.

2 cups all-purpose flour
1½ teaspoons baking powder
1 teaspoon ground ginger
1 teaspoon ground cinnamon
½ teaspoon ground nutmeg
½ teaspoon salt
½ cup butter, softened
1 cup sugar
2 eggs
1¼ cups milk
2½ cups diced mixed candied fruits and peels
Powdered Sugar Icing

1. Grease and flour a 2½-quart heatproof bowl; set aside. In a small bowl stir together 1¾ cups of the flour, the baking powder, ginger, cinnamon, nutmeg, and salt; set aside.
2. In a large mixing bowl beat butter on medium to high 30 seconds. Beat in sugar until combined. Add eggs, one at a time, beating on low. Alternately add flour mixture and milk, beating on low. Toss together 2 cups of the candied fruit with remaining ¾ cup flour. Stir into beaten mixture. Pour into prepared bowl. Cover with greased foil, folding the foil over the edge and pressing against side of bowl.
3. Place bowl on rack* in Dutch oven; add water 1 inch up sides of bowl. Cover; bring water to boiling. Reduce to simmering. Steam 1¾ to 2 hours or until a wooden skewer inserted in center comes out clean. Check water level every 30 minutes or so and add boiling water as needed.
4. Carefully remove bowl from Dutch oven; remove foil. Let stand for 10 minutes; unmold onto a serving plate. Cool for 30 minutes. Drizzle with Powdered Sugar Icing and top with remaining candied fruit and peels. Serve warm or at room temperature. Makes 12 servings.
Powdered Sugar Icing: In a small bowl combine 1 cup powdered sugar and enough milk (4 to 5 teaspoons) to make an icing of drizzling consistency.
***Test Kitchen Tip:** If you do not have a rack that will fit inside your Dutch oven, place a few canning lid rings in the bottom of your Dutch oven so the bowl will stand flat on top of them.

CITRUS MOCK MIMOSAS

Ham-Asparagus Strata

This cheesy strata makes a great brunch dish because you can assemble it the night before and bake it in the morning. Pictured on page 101.

4 English muffins, torn or cut into bite-size pieces (4 cups)
2 cups cubed cooked ham
1 10-ounce package frozen cut asparagus or frozen cut broccoli, thawed and well drained, or 2 cups cut-up fresh asparagus or broccoli
4 ounces process Swiss cheese, torn, or process Gruyère cheese, cut up
4 beaten eggs
¼ cup sour cream
1¼ cups milk
2 tablespoons finely chopped onion
1 tablespoon Dijon mustard
⅛ teaspoon ground black pepper

1. In a greased 2-quart square baking dish layer half of the English muffin pieces. Top with the ham, asparagus, and cheese. Top with the remaining English muffin pieces.
2. In a medium bowl whisk together the eggs and sour cream. Stir in milk, onion, mustard, and pepper. Pour evenly over the layers in dish. Cover and chill for 2 to 24 hours.
3. Preheat oven to 325°F. Bake, uncovered, for 60 to 65 minutes or until the internal temperature registers 170°F on an instant-read thermometer. Let stand for 10 minutes before serving. Makes 6 to 8 servings.

Citrus Mock Mimosas

The fresh, fruity flavors of citrus make this the perfect cocktail for a brunch. You can also use tangerines, tangelos, and blood oranges, which are readily available. Fresh pineapple wedges make a festive garnish.

1½ cups fresh orange juice
1 cup fresh grapefruit juice
½ cup fresh lime juice
2 to 4 tablespoons honey
2 12-ounce bottles sparkling water, chilled
Pineapple wedges

1. In a 4-cup glass measure combine orange juice, grapefruit juice, lime juice, and honey. Stir until honey is dissolved. Cover and chill mixture for at least 2 hours or up to 24 hours to blend flavors.
2. To serve, pour juice mixture into four champagne glasses. Add sparkling water and stir lightly to mix. If desired, garnish each serving with a pineapple wedge. Makes 8 (¾-cup) servings.

Triple Berry Salad

Strawberries, raspberries, and blueberries burst with color and make for the most spectacular brunch salad. A refreshing cream of coconut dressing gives this an unexpected twist.

6 cups coarsely chopped romaine lettuce
3 cups quartered fresh strawberries
½ cup fresh raspberries
½ cup fresh blueberrries
¼ cup cream of coconut
2 tablespoons lemon juice
1 tablespoon water
1 tablespoon Dijon mustard
½ teaspoon ground ginger
Salt
Black pepper

1. Place lettuce in an extra-large bowl Top with strawberries, raspberries, and blueberries. If desired, cover and chill for up to 1 hour.
2. For dressing, in a small bowl whisk together cream of coconut, lemon juice, the water, mustard, and ginger. Season to taste with salt and pepper. If desired, cover and chill until serving time.
3. To serve, pour dressing over salad; toss gently to coat. Makes 6 to 8 servings.

TRIPLE BERRY SALAD

EASY CHOCOLATE-ALMOND CROISSANTS

Easy Chocolate-Almond Croissants

Dark chocolate, almond paste, and whipping cream make a rich filling for packaged crescent roll dough used in this simple sweet bread.

- ½ of an 8-ounce can almond paste, cut into small pieces
- ¼ cup whipping cream
- 4 ounces dark baking chocolate, chopped
- 1 8-ounce package refrigerated crescent rolls (8)
- 1 egg, lightly beaten
- 1 tablespoon water
- ¼ cup sliced almonds
- 1 tablespoon powdered sugar

1. Preheat oven to 350°F. Lightly grease a baking sheet; set aside. For filling, in a medium bowl combine almond paste and 1 tablespoon of the cream. Beat with an electric mixer on medium until mixture is nearly smooth. Add the remaining cream, 1 tablespoon at a time, beating until nearly smooth. Stir in chocolate.

2. Unroll crescent roll dough and separate at perforations into eight triangles. Spoon filling onto wide ends of dough triangles; spread slightly. Starting at the wide end of each triangle, roll up dough around filling toward the point. Place croissants, point sides down, on prepared baking sheet; curve the ends.

3. In a small bowl combine egg and the water. Brush dough lightly with egg mixture; sprinkle with almonds.

4. Bake for 15 to 17 minutes or until golden brown. Transfer to a wire rack; cool slightly. Sprinkle lightly with powdered sugar. Serve warm. Makes 8 croissants.

To Make Ahead: Prepare and bake as directed; cool completely. Place croissants in a single layer in an airtight container; cover. Store at room temperature for up to 3 days. Just before serving, preheat oven to 350°F. Arrange croissants on an ungreased baking sheet. Bake for 5 to 6 minutes or until warm.

SPICED CHAI PUNCH

Spiced Chai Punch

Instead of the usual coffee, warm up your brunch with a steaming spiced milk-and-tea blend, a drink that's especially soothing on a chilly winter morning.

- 6 cups water
- 2 teaspoons fennel seeds
- 12 whole cloves
- ½ teaspoon whole cardamom pods
- 2 4-inch cinnamon sticks
- 2 2-inch slices fresh ginger
- ⅓ cup Darjeeling tea leaves
- 2 cups milk
- ½ cup raw sugar or granulated sugar
- Orange peel strips (optional)
- Cinnamon sticks, crushed (optional)*

1. In a large saucepan combine the water, fennel seeds, cloves, cardamom, the 4-inch cinnamon sticks, and ginger. Bring to boiling; reduce heat. Simmer, covered, for 15 minutes.

2. Remove saucepan from heat; add tea leaves. Cover and allow to steep for 30 minutes.

3. Strain mixture through a fine-mesh sieve; return to saucepan. Add milk and sugar. Cook and stir over medium heat until sugar dissolves.

4. Pour punch into heatproof cups or glasses. If desired, garnish each serving with orange peel strips and crushed cinnamon. Makes 8 (8-ounce) servings.

***Test Kitchen Tip:** If you don't have time to crush the cinnamon, add a stick to each drink for flavorful stirring.

HERB-BACON RIB ROAST
Recipe on page 108

Feast to Impress

A succulent centerpiece roast, a dazzling dessert, and other delicious surprises make this year's gathering the absolute best.

HAZELNUT-PUMPKIN CHEESECAKE
Recipe on page 108

Herb-Bacon Rib Roast

This roast is ideal for celebrations and Sunday dinners. It's a costly cut, but worth it because it does not require a lot of care or spices to make it great. Vegetables are cooked alongside the roast for a flavorful one-pan meal. Pictured on page 106.

- 1 recipe Herb-Bacon Topper
- 1 4- to 5-pound beef rib roast (chin bone removed)
- 1 teaspoon cracked black peppercorns
- ½ teaspoon salt
- 1 pound baby carrots with tops, trimmed
- 1 pound small red potatoes (halve any large potatoes)
- 1 pound purple boiling onions, halved
- 3 to 4 cups baby spinach
- 1 15-ounce can butter beans, rinsed and drained

1. Prepare Herb-Bacon Topper. Preheat oven to 350°F. Sprinkle beef roast with cracked pepper, salt, and half of the Herb-Bacon Topper (refrigerate remaining topper and reserved bacon pieces until ready to use). Place meat, bone side down, in a shallow roasting pan. Insert an oven-safe meat thermometer into center of roast.
2. Roast, uncovered, for 45 minutes. Arrange carrots, potatoes, and onions around roast and toss to gently coat. Roast, uncovered, for 1 to 1¼ hours more or until meat thermometer registers 135°F for medium-rare. Sprinkle meat with remaining Herb-Bacon Topper; cover and let stand for 15 minutes. Temperature of meat after standing should be 145°F. Push meat and carrots to one side of pan. Stir spinach and beans into drippings in other side of pan; sprinkle with reserved bacon pieces. Makes 10 servings.
Herb-Bacon Topper: Cook 4 slices bacon until crisp; drain on paper towels. Chop half the bacon; stir in 1 tablespoon chopped fresh thyme and 1½ teaspoons chopped fresh rosemary. Break remaining half of the bacon into pieces to sprinkle into the spinach and beans before serving.

Hazelnut-Pumpkin Cheesecake

Combine two classic desserts—pumpkin pie and cheesecake—to create an impressive do-ahead dessert. Everyone will love the creamy, rich filling and warmly spiced gingersnap crust.
Pictured on page 107.

- 24 gingersnaps
- 2 tablespoons granulated sugar
- ¼ cup unsalted butter, melted
- 2 8-ounce packages cream cheese, softened
- 5 eggs
- 1 15-ounce can pumpkin
- ¾ cup packed brown sugar
- ½ cup hazelnut liqueur
- 1 teaspoon ground cinnamon
- 1 teaspoon vanilla
- ½ teaspoon ground ginger
- ¼ teaspoon grated whole nutmeg
- ¼ teaspoon ground cloves
- 1 16-ounce carton sour cream
- ¼ cup granulated sugar
- ¼ cup hazelnut liqueur
- ½ cup hazelnuts (filberts), coarsely chopped*

1. For crust, in a food processor combine gingersnaps and the 2 tablespoons granulated sugar. Cover and process to form fine crumbs. With processor running, slowly add melted butter, processing until combined. Press mixture evenly onto the bottom of a 9-inch springform pan. Chill until firm.
2. Meanwhile, preheat oven to 350°F. Place cream cheese in food processor. Cover and process until smooth. Add eggs, pumpkin, brown sugar, the ½ cup liqueur, the cinnamon, vanilla, ginger, nutmeg, and cloves. Cover and process until smooth, stopping once to scrape sides of bowl. Pour filling over crust, spreading evenly.
3. Place springform pan in a shallow baking pan. Bake for 40 to 45 minutes or until edge is firm and center appears nearly set when gently shaken.
4. Meanwhile, for topping, in a medium bowl combine sour cream, the ¼ cup granulated sugar, and the ¼ cup liqueur. Transfer to a measuring cup with a lip. Without removing cheesecake from oven, pour topping over cheesecake, spreading evenly. Bake for 8 to 10 minutes more or until edge of topping just starts to bubble. Cool completely in pan on a wire rack. Cover loosely and chill for at least 12 hours.
5. To serve, loosen edge of cheesecake from sides of pan; remove sides of pan. Cut cheesecake while it is still chilled and firm. Let stand at room temperature for 20 minutes before serving. Sprinkle with hazelnuts. Makes 12 servings.

Spinach, Pear, and Shaved Parmesan Salad

Let the cheese soften at room temperature before shaving it with a vegetable peeler. Wrap the cheese shavings in plastic wrap until ready to use.

- 8 cups fresh baby spinach
- 2 Bosc pears, quartered lengthwise, cored, and thinly sliced
- 2 ounces Parmesan or Parmigiano-Reggiano cheese, shaved
- 2 tablespoons balsamic vinegar
- 1 tablespoon whole-grain mustard
- 1 teaspoon sugar
- 1 teaspoon salt
- ¼ teaspoon freshly ground black pepper
- ½ cup extra virgin olive oil

1. In a large bowl toss together spinach, pears, and cheese. For dressing whisk together vinegar, mustard, sugar, salt, and pepper. Whisk in oil. Drizzle on salad and pass remaining. Makes 8 servings.

***Toast the chopped hazelnuts to enhance the flavor of the cheesecake. Place the nuts in a large skillet. Cook over medium-low heat, shaking the skillet often for 7 to 10 minutes or until skins begin to flake and the nuts are light golden brown.**

SPINACH, PEAR, AND SHAVED PARMESAN SALAD

APRICOT-SAGE LOAVES

Apricot-Sage Loaves

You can freeze the loaves once they've been baked. Place in an airtight container and freeze for up to 1 month. Thaw at room temperature and warm in a 350°F oven for 8 to 10 minutes before serving.

- ½ cup onion, chopped (1 medium)
- 1 tablespoon olive oil
- ¾ cup warm water (105 to 115°F)
- 1 package active dry yeast
- ½ cup milk
- 2 tablespoons sugar
- 2 tablespoons butter
- 1 teaspoon salt
- ½ cup dried apricots, finely snipped
- ½ cup shredded Swiss cheese (2 ounces)
- 1 tablespoon fresh sage, snipped
- 2½ cups all-purpose flour
- Nonstick cooking spray or olive oil
- Cornmeal
- 1 egg
- 2 teaspoons water
- Fresh sage leaves

1. Cook onion in hot olive oil over medium heat about 4 minutes or until tender. Set aside.

2. In a large bowl stir together the warm water and yeast. Let stand for 5 minutes. Meanwhile, in a small saucepan heat and stir milk, sugar, butter, salt, cooked onion, apricots, Swiss cheese, and sage just until warm (120°F to 130°F) and butter almost melts. Stir milk mixture into yeast mixture until combined. Stir in flour (dough will be sticky). Lightly coat a medium bowl with cooking spray; transfer dough to the greased bowl. Lightly coat a sheet of plastic wrap with cooking spray; cover bowl with the greased plastic wrap and chill overnight.

3. Using a dough scraper or spatula, carefully loosen dough from bowl and turn out onto a floured surface. Cover with the greased plastic wrap and let stand for 30 minutes.

4. Grease a baking sheet; sprinkle lightly with cornmeal. Gently shape dough into three 3½-inch round loaves. Transfer to the prepared baking sheet, using dough scraper or spatula if necessary. Cover and let rise in a warm place until nearly double in size (about 1 hour).

5. Preheat oven to 400°F. In a small bowl whisk together egg and 2 teaspoons water; brush over loaves. If desired, top loaves with a few small fresh sage leaves. Bake about 20 minutes or until an instant-read thermometer inserted in each loaf registers at least 200°F. If necessary, cover loaves with foil during the last 5 minutes of baking to prevent overbrowning.

6. Remove from baking sheet; cool on a wire rack. Makes 3 (3½-inch) loaves.

MASHED SWEET POTATOES WITH WHITE CHEDDAR

Mashed Sweet Potatoes with White Cheddar

Bourbon adds a buttery bite to this impressive side dish, and cream and white cheddar add richness. Get a head start by roasting the sweet potatoes the day before your celebration.

- 3 pounds sweet potatoes (about 7 medium)
- ¼ cup butter
- 1 teaspoon kosher salt or salt
- 3 ounces aged white cheddar cheese, shredded
- ¼ cup bourbon or orange juice
- ¼ cup whipping cream
- ¼ cup packed dark brown sugar
- 1 large red onion, cut into thin wedges
- 2 medium red apples, cored and cut into wedges
- 2 teaspoons snipped fresh thyme
- ¼ teaspoon black pepper

1. Preheat oven to 425°F. Scrub potatoes and prick with fork; place on foil-lined baking sheet. Bake for 40 minutes or until tender. Reduce oven temperature to 325°F.

2. When potatoes are cool enough to handle, scrape pulp from skin. Transfer to bowl. Mash with 2 tablespoons of the butter and ¾ teaspoon of the salt. Stir in cheese, bourbon, cream, and 2 tablespoons of the brown sugar. Transfer to buttered 1½-quart casserole. Bake, covered, for 30 minutes or until heated through.

3. Meanwhile, in microwave-safe 2-quart casserole combine remaining butter, brown sugar, and salt. Add onion. Microwave on 100% power (high) for 3 to 4 minutes or until onion is crisp-tender. Add apples. Cover and microwave for 2 minutes more or until apple is tender. Stir in thyme and pepper. Transfer sweet potatoes to a serving bowl; top with apple mixture. Makes 8 servings.

Candy Delights

From rich chocolate decadence to sweet, buttery crunch, you'll be hard-pressed to find store-bought candies as tempting as these homemade renditions.

CRÈME DE MENTHE CUPS
Recipe on page 114

CHOCOLATE BONBON POPS
Recipe on page 114

Crème de Menthe Cups

A crispy cookie crust made of graham crackers and cocoa powder pairs with a rich, minty filling. Pictured on page 112.

1½ cups powdered sugar
¼ cup unsweetened cocoa powder
2 tablespoons whipping cream
1 teaspoon vanilla
¼ cup butter, softened
¾ cup crushed graham crackers
1 3-ounce package cream cheese, softened
2 tablespoons butter, softened
1 cup powdered sugar
1 tablespoon crème de menthe
White chocolate, mint chocolate, or milk chocolate curls (optional)

1. Line twenty-four 1¾-inch muffin cups with paper or foil liners; set aside. In a small bowl stir together the 1½ cups powdered sugar and the cocoa powder; set aside. In another small bowl stir together whipping cream and vanilla; set aside.
2. In a medium mixing bowl beat the ¼ cup butter with an electric mixer on medium to high for 30 seconds. Alternately beat in powdered sugar and whipping cream mixtures on low until combined. Beat in crushed graham crackers.
3. Shape dough into 1-inch balls; place balls in prepared muffin cups. Press dough evenly against bottom and sides of each cup. Chill for 1 hour.
4. For filling, in a medium mixing bowl beat cream cheese and the 2 tablespoons butter with an electric mixer on medium to high for 30 seconds. Gradually beat in the 1 cup powdered sugar and the creme de menthe. Spoon or pipe filling into chocolate cups. If desired, garnish with chocolate curls. Cover and chill for at least 4 hours before serving. Makes 24 candies.
To Store: Place cups in a single layer in an airtight container; cover. Store in the refrigerator for up to 3 days

Chocolate Bonbon Pops

Find lollipop sticks for these no-bake candies in the baking section of large supermarkets and baking supply stores. Pictured on page 113.

18 chocolate sandwich cookies with cream filling
1½ cups pecans, toasted
2 tablespoons orange liqueur or orange juice
1 tablespoon light-color corn syrup
2 tablespoons unsweetened cocoa powder

20 lollipop sticks
1 12-ounce package milk chocolate or semisweet chocolate pieces
1 tablespoon shortening
Red and green candies and/or sprinkles

1. In large food processor bowl combine cookies and ¾ cup of the nuts; pulse until cookies are crushed. Add orange liqueur, corn syrup, and cocoa powder; process until combined. Add remaining nuts; pulse until coarsely chopped.
2. Line a large baking sheet with parchment paper. Shape cookie mixture in 1-inch balls. Place on baking sheet, insert a lollipop stick, and freeze for 30 minutes.
3. In a small saucepan combine chocolate pieces and shortening. Cook and stir over medium-low heat just until melted. Remove from heat. Dip pops in chocolate and desired candies. Return to baking sheet. Loosely cover and refrigerate 1 hour or until chocolate is set. If using liqueur, flavor will mellow after a day or two. Makes 20 pops.
To Store: Place candies in a single layer in an airtight container; cover and refrigerate for up to 1 week.

Candied Cherry Opera Fudge

2 cups sugar
½ cup milk
½ cup half-and-half or light cream
1 tablespoon light-color corn syrup
½ teaspoon salt
1 tablespoon butter
1 teaspoon vanilla
⅓ cup coarsely chopped candied red cherries
Halved candied red cherries (optional)

1. Line a 5¾×3×2-inch loaf pan with foil, extending foil over the edges of the pan. Butter the foil; set aside.
2. Butter the sides of a heavy 2-quart saucepan. In the saucepan combine the sugar, milk, half-and-half, corn syrup, and salt. Cook over medium heat, stirring constantly, until sugar dissolves and mixture comes to a boil. Clip a candy thermometer to sides of pan.
3. Continue boiling at a moderate, steady rate, stirring occasionally, until candy thermometer registers 236°F, soft ball stage (about 20 minutes). Adjust heat as necessary to maintain a steady boil.
4. Remove saucepan from heat. Add butter and vanilla but do not stir. Cool, without stirring, to 170°F (about 20 minutes). Remove thermometer from saucepan. Beat mixture vigorously with a wooden spoon for 5 minutes. Add ⅓ cup cherries. Beat mixture vigorously for 1 minute more. Pour into prepared pan, spreading evenly. Let stand until firm. Use foil to lift fudge from pan; remove foil. To serve, top with additional cherries. Cut fudge into thick slices. Makes 20 servings.

Lemon Drop Bark

Melt the candy coating and baking chocolate, add the crushed candy, and you're done. The crushed lemon drops give this sweet treat some pucker.

1 pound vanilla-flavor candy coating, cut up
6 ounces white baking chocolate, coarsely chopped
¾ cup finely crushed lemon drops, peppermint candy canes, or fruit-flavor hard candy (about 6 ounces)
¼ cup finely chopped pistachios, macadamia nuts, or slivered almonds

1. Line a large baking sheet with foil; set aside. In a heavy medium saucepan heat candy coating and white baking chocolate over low heat, stirring frequently until melted and smooth. Remove from heat. Stir in ½ cup of the crushed candy.
2. Pour mixture onto the prepared baking sheet, spreading to about ⅜-inch thickness. Sprinkle with remaining crushed candy and pistachios; press slightly. Chill about 30 minutes or until firm. (Or let candy stand at room temperature for several hours until firm.)
3. Carefully peel candy off foil and break into pieces. Makes 1¾ pounds or about 36 (2-inch) pieces.
To Store: Layer pieces of candy between waxed paper in an airtight container; cover. Store in the refrigerator for up to 2 weeks or freeze for up to 3 months.

LEMON DROP BARK

MOCHA FUDGE

Mocha Fudge

This soft and oh-so-sweet coffee-flavored fudge is prepared the old-fashioned way with careful temperature monitoring and lots of beating by hand to achieve the perfect texture.

2 cups granulated sugar
1 cup half-and-half or light cream
½ cup packed brown sugar
½ cup unsweetened cocoa powder
2 tablespoons instant coffee crystals
2 tablespoons light-color corn syrup
2 tablespoons butter
¼ teaspoon salt
2 teaspoons vanilla
½ cup chopped chocolate-covered coffee beans (optional)
Canned chocolate frosting (optional)
Chocolate-covered coffee beans, halved (optional)

1. Line an 8×8×2-inch baking pan with foil, extending the foil over edges of pan. Butter foil; set pan aside.
2. Butter the sides of a 3-quart heavy saucepan. In the saucepan combine granulated sugar, half-and-half, brown sugar, cocoa powder, coffee crystals, corn syrup, butter, and salt. Cook and stir over medium heat until mixture is boiling. Clip a candy thermometer to the side of the pan. Reduce heat to medium-low; continue boiling at a moderate, steady rate, stirring occasionally, until thermometer registers 236°F, soft-ball stage (about 25 minutes). (Adjust heat as necessary to maintain a steady boil.)
3. Remove saucepan from heat. Add vanilla, but do not stir. Cool, without stirring, to 110°F (50 to 60 minutes). Remove thermometer from saucepan. Beat mixture vigorously with a clean wooden spoon just until candy starts to thicken. Continue beating just until fudge starts to lose its gloss (6 to 8 minutes total). If desired, quickly fold in ½ cup chopped coffee beans.
4. Immediately spread fudge evenly in the prepared pan. Score fudge into squares while warm. Let fudge cool to room temperature. When fudge is firm, use the edges of the foil to lift fudge from pan. Cut into squares. If desired, pipe or spoon a little chocolate frosting onto each square and top with a halved coffee bean. Makes 64 pieces.
To Store: Layer fudge between sheets of waxed paper in an airtight container; cover. Store at room temperature for up to 1 week.

ORANGE AND NUT TOFFEE

Orange and Nut Toffee Sticks

The zing of candied orange peel balances the combination of crunchy cashews and walnuts in this sweet, buttery brittle. Form the gorgeous sticks by shaping a piece of heavy-duty foil to hold the candy.

⅔ cup coarsely chopped cashews
⅔ cup coarsely chopped walnuts, toasted
1 cup butter
1 cup sugar
3 tablespoons water
1 tablespoon light-color corn syrup
1 cup purchased candied orange peel, coarsely chopped

1. Layer two 12×12-inch squares of heavy duty foil. Pinch up foil every 1½ inches to form raised edges, making four long troughs to pour the toffee into. Fold up edges and ends. Place on a rimmed baking pan. Divide ⅓ cup cashews and ⅓ cup walnuts among the four troughs. Set aside.
2. In a 2-quart heavy saucepan melt butter over low heat. Stir in sugar, the water, and corn syrup. Bring to boiling over medium-high heat, stirring until sugar is dissolved. Avoid splashing side of saucepan. Clip a candy thermometer to side of pan. Cook over medium heat, stirring frequently, until thermometer registers 290°F, soft-crack stage (about 12 to 15 minutes). Mixture should boil at a moderate, steady rate with bubbles over entire surface. (Adjust heat as necessary to maintain a steady boil and watch temperature carefully during the last 5 minutes of cooking because temperature can increase quickly at the end.) Remove from heat; remove thermometer.
3. Carefully pour corn syrup mixture into the four troughs; sprinkle with remaining nuts and the candied orange peel. Let stand at room temperature for several hours. Peel back the foil to pull up the toffee sticks. Makes 4 sticks.
To Store: Layer toffee sticks between sheets of waxed paper in an airtight container; cover. Store at room temperature for up to 2 weeks.

In-a-Twinkling

popcorn fun

▲ Candied Popcorn Balls

Prepare your favorite popcorn ball recipe, adding a few drops of green food coloring to mixture and stirring in candy-coated red and green milk chocolate pieces. Shape the mixture into 3- or 4-inch-diameter balls and wrap each in plastic wrap. Store at room temperature for up to 1 week.

Sweet 'n' Salty Snack Mix ▶

Pop a batch of popcorn; place in a large bowl. Toss in your favorite holiday munchies and candies, including star- or Christmas tree-shape pretzels, red and/or green candy-coated peanut-flavor or milk chocolate pieces, and assorted gumdrops. Store in an airtight container at room temperature for up to 3 days.

Chocolate Clusters

Preheat oven to 275°F. Grease a large shallow roasting pan. Combine 12 cups popped popcorn and ½ cup sunflower kernels. In a large saucepan combine ½ cup butter and 4 ounces semisweet chocolate, chopped. Heat and stir over medium-low heat until melted. Add 30 large marshmallows; heat and stir until melted and smooth. Remove from heat. Stir in 1 teaspoon vanilla. Pour chocolate mixture over popcorn mixture; stir to coat. Spread mixture into prepared pan. Bake about 20 minutes or until crisp, stirring once. Cool in pan on a wire rack. Break mixture into pieces.

Red Hot Ornaments

Prepare your favorite popcorn ball recipe, stirring in red cinnamon candies and shaping mixture into 3- to 4-inch-diameter balls. Decorate balls with small gumdrops and shoestring licorice, attaching candies with a small amount of canned white frosting. Wrap each ball in plastic wrap. Store at room temperature for up to 1 week.

Snow Much Fun

Start with your favorite popcorn ball recipe. Stack two balls together; secure with frosting. Push pretzel-stick arms into sides; add jawbreaker eyes and buttons, a candy corn nose, a mini jawbreaker smile, and fruit leather scarf. For the hat, dip half of a large marshmallow and a chocolate wafer cookie sandwich into melted chocolate; freeze until set.

ifts

Handcrafted holiday surprises, wrapped in delightful papers and bows, make the season oh-so-bright.

Quick Fix

A pretty sticker is all it takes to jazz up a plain glass votive. Choose a beaded beauty to add dimension.

Holders of Light

In the wink of an eye you can make an array of candles for all the lucky ones on your holiday gift list.

Sew Nice

A few trims from the sewing room transform an ordinary votive candleholder into a festive accent. Use a low-temp glue gun to secure a narrow ribbon around the top portion of the candleholder. Cover the seam with layered buttons, the larger edged with metallic chenille stem.

Razzle Dazzle

Choose a glitter color that blends with the gift recipient's holiday decor and drench a candle cup in it. Brush decoupage medium onto the outside of the cup and, while wet, sprinkle with glitter. When dry, tie a coordinating bow around the cup.

Garlands Aglow

A glittered pillar candle gets extra shine wrapped in a sea of colorful beaded garland. Hold the arrangement together in a large glass dish that's slightly shorter than the candle. You can get a similar look with individual beads or metallic jingle bells.

North Pole Village

Talk about the cutest gift wrap idea in town! Give presents unforgettable wraps by making them look like buildings all decked out for the Christmas season.

A

B

C

D

House Boxes

WHAT YOU NEED

Wrapping or decorative scrapbook papers
Decorative cardstock
Scissors
Tape
White jumbo rickrack
Trims, such as adhesive jewels, ribbon, and metallic chenille stems
Hot-glue and glue sticks

WHAT YOU DO

1. Wrap gift boxes with wrapping or decorative scrapbook paper as shown in Photo A, securing on the back with tape. If desired, combine two boxes for added dimension. To enable the boxes to stand, use those that are deep enough to do so without support.

2. Using the photo for ideas, cut a triangular roof from decorative cardstock. Glue white rickrack to the edges of the back side to resemble snow from the front as shown in Photo B. Cut out building details such as windows, doors, and chimneys from paper; glue roof and other building details in place. Define building details with trims as shown in Photos C and D.

3. To make trees, shape papers into small cones, trimming as necessary and taping seams to secure. Decorate cones with trims to appear as tiny Christmas trees.

Holiday Wishes

Decked Out

Go ahead—make a scene, a holiday scene, on towels for the bath or kitchen. Cut out the desired design from holiday fabric, trimming into a rectangle for a hand towel or into a band for a bath towel. Fold under the edges ¼ inch; press. Sewing ⅛ inch from the edge, machine-stitch the scene onto contrasting fabric. Trim edges along border, turn under, and press. Pin design to towel and stitch around edges. To add edging, cut a strip of fabric 2 inches wide and long enough to fit short towel edge. Fold under ¼ inch along each long edge; press. Machine- or hand-sew to towel edge.

Timeless Towels

Classic or vintage, playful or traditional, fabric transforms plain towels into seasonal sensations.

Merry Mug

Paint a bright-eyed Christmas character that struts her stuff across a good-morning coffee mug.

Java Jessie

Like paint-by-number, this cute bird is super simple to paint, no matter what your skill level.

WHAT YOU NEED

Blue, green, bright pink, white, and black glass paints
White glass or ceramic coffee mug
Paper plate
Paintbrushes

WHAT YOU DO

1. Using the patterns on page 157 and Photo A as a guide, paint a large blue paisley on one side of the mug; let dry.

2. Blending green in with the blue, paint a paisley wing, two stick legs, and heart-shape tail feathers as shown in Photo B.

3. Paint feet as in Photo C. Blending bright pink and white, make short vertical stripes at the top of the bird's head as shown in Photo C.

4. Paint a hat in bright pink, adding a blended white and pink tassel at the tip as shown in Photo D. When hat is dry, dip paintbrush handle in white and dot hat.

5. Paint a yellow beak. Make eyes by dipping a small paintbrush handle into black paint and dot where shown in photograph.

6. Using short black strokes, outline the shapes as shown.

7. Blend blue and white and paint dime-size rings of snow in the background; let dry. Cure the paint as directed by the manufacturer.

Sweet Delivery

With a little bit of holiday bliss in every bite, these beautifully packaged cookie gifts are one of the sweetest ways to say "Happy Holidays!"

Raising the Bar

Scrapbook supplies create a fun look. Using the pattern on page 155, cut out the shape from decorative cardstock; fold as directed. Punch holes through the layers and insert decorative brads to secure. Place the box in a cellophane bag, stack bars inside, and tie with a ribbon. Hot-glue a bell to the bow.

CHRISTMAS BLONDIES

PEPPERMINT SANDWICH CRÈMES

Cookie Roll

Share a sleeve of cookies lined up neatly in clear cellophane. Cut cellophane 8 inches longer than the stack and wide enough to overlap a couple inches. Tape cellophane around cookie stack. To make ties, thread two miniature plastic ornaments on each of four 8-inch-long strands of elastic cord; knot ends separately. Use two ties on each end of cellophane.

Christmas Blondies

Fruitcake ingredients—brandy, candied cherries, and walnuts—punch up the flavor of these bar cookies.

- ⅔ cup butter, softened
- 2 cups packed brown sugar
- 2 large eggs
- 1 tablespoon cherry brandy or cherry juice (optional)
- 1½ teaspoons baking powder
- 2 teaspoons vanilla
- ¼ teaspoon salt
- 2¼ cups all-purpose flour
- 1 cup chopped walnuts, toasted*
- ¾ cup chopped white or dark sweet chocolate
- ½ cup coarsely chopped candied cherries

1. Preheat oven to 350°F. Lightly grease a 13×9×2-inch baking pan.
2. In a large mixing bowl beat butter on medium for 30 seconds. Add brown sugar; beat until well combined. Beat in eggs, brandy, baking powder, vanilla, and salt. Add flour; beat just until blended. Stir in nuts, chocolate, and cherries. Spread in prepared pan.
3. Bake for 30 minutes or until golden. Cool completely in pan on wire rack. Cut into bars. Makes 24 bars.
To Store: Layer bars between sheets of waxed paper in an airtight container; cover. Store at room temperature for up to 3 days or freeze for up to 3 months.

***Test Kitchen Tip:** To toast nuts, spread them in a shallow pan. Bake in a 350°F oven for 5 to 10 minutes or until light brown, shaking the pan once or twice.

Peppermint Sandwich Crèmes

Crushed peppermint candies add a refreshing crunch to these buttery gems. Place the candies in a resealable plastic bag and, using a meat mallet, pound the candies lightly.

- ½ cup butter, softened
- 1 cup sugar
- ¼ teaspoon baking soda
- ¼ teaspoon salt
- 1 egg
- 2 teaspoons vanilla
- 1 teaspoon peppermint extract
- 1¾ cups all-purpose flour
- 1 recipe Peppermint-Cream Cheese Filling
- Finely crushed peppermint candies or sprinkles

1. In a large bowl beat butter with an electric mixer on medium to high for 30 seconds. Add sugar, baking soda, and salt. Beat until combined, scraping bowl occasionally. Beat in egg, vanilla, and peppermint extract until combined.
2. Beat in as much of the flour as you can with the mixer. Using a wooden spoon, stir in any remaining flour. Divide dough into four portions. Shape each portion into an 8-inch roll. Wrap each roll in plastic wrap or waxed paper. Freeze for 2 to 3 hours or until dough is firm enough to slice.
3. Preheat oven to 350°F. Unwrap rolls and cut into ⅜-inch slices. Place slices 1 inch apart on an ungreased cookie sheet. Bake for 10 to 12 minutes or just until firm. Transfer cookies to a wire rack; cool.
4. Spread Peppermint-Cream Cheese Filling on bottoms of half of the cookies, spreading to edges. Top with the remaining cookies, bottom sides down. Press lightly until filling comes just slightly over edges. Roll edges of cookies in crushed candies or sprinkles. Makes 35 sandwich cookies.
Peppermint-Cream Cheese Filling: In a bowl combine one 3-ounce package softened cream cheese and ¼ cup softened butter. Beat with an electric mixer on medium until smooth. Beat in 1 teaspoon vanilla and ½ teaspoon peppermint extract. Gradually beat in 3 cups powdered sugar. If necessary, beat in enough milk, 1 teaspoon at a time, to make filling spreading consistency. Makes 1⅔ cups.
To Store: Layer filled cookies between sheets of waxed paper in an airtight container; cover. Store at room temperature for up to 3 days or freeze for up to 3 months.

Button Tree

A lunch bag makes the perfect packaging for a stack of bars. To trim it, start by hot-gluing a brown-button tree trunk centered at bottom. Complete shape with stacked red and white buttons. To give a stitched-on look, use embroidery thread to make an X before gluing. Insert bars, fold over the bag top, punch two holes, and tie with cord.

VANILLA AND MOCHA ANGEL WINGS

Trimmed Tray
Use odds and ends of sewing trims to give a paper plate an unforgettable edge. Hot-glue a trim along the plate's edge and add a second layer on the underside.

Maple-Nut Pie Bars

Infuse the rich flavor of maple syrup into a bar that falls somewhere between a pie and a cookie. A thick layer of nuts on top and a crumbly shortbread crust on the bottom make this an indulgent treat.

- Nonstick cooking spray
- 1¼ cups all-purpose flour
- ½ cup powdered sugar
- ¼ teaspoon salt
- ½ cup butter, cut up
- 2 eggs, lightly beaten
- 1 cup chopped mixed nuts or pecans
- ½ cup packed brown sugar
- ½ cup pure maple syrup
- 2 tablespoons butter, melted
- ½ teaspoon maple flavoring or 1 teaspoon vanilla

1. Preheat oven to 350°F. Line a 11×7×1½-inch baking pan with foil, extending foil over the edges of pan. Lightly coat foil with cooking spray; set aside.

2. For crust, in a medium bowl stir together flour, powdered sugar, and salt. Using a pastry blender, cut in the ½ cup butter until mixture resembles coarse crumbs. Press mixture evenly onto the bottom of prepared baking pan. Bake about 20 minutes or until lightly browned.

3. Meanwhile, for filling, in a medium bowl combine eggs, mixed nuts, brown sugar, maple syrup, the 2 tablespoons melted butter, and maple flavoring. Spread filling evenly over hot crust.

4. Bake about 20 minutes more or until filling is set. Cool in pan on a wire rack. Using the edges of the foil, lift the baked mixture out of the pan. Cut into bars. Makes 24 bars.

To Store: Place bars in a single layer in an airtight container; cover. Store in the refrigerator for up to 2 days.

Vanilla Angel Wings

These divine cookies taste so good, your spirits will rise to new heights with just one bite. What's more, they look lovely piled on a red cookie platter.

- 1 cup butter, softened
- ½ cup powdered sugar
- 4 teaspoons vanilla
- ¼ teaspoon salt
- 2⅓ cups all-purpose flour
- Powdered sugar

1. Line two baking sheets with parchment; set aside. In a large mixing bowl beat butter on medium to high for 30 seconds. Add ½ cup powdered sugar, the vanilla, and salt; beat mixture until well combined. Beat in as much flour as you can. Stir in any remaining flour with a wooden spoon. If necessary, cover and chill dough for 30 minutes or until easy to handle.

2. Preheat oven to 400°F. Shape dough into 1-inch balls, then pinch and shape balls into crescents. Place 2 inches apart on prepared baking sheets.

3. Bake for 12 to 13 minutes or until bottoms are golden brown. Cool for 1 minute on sheets. Transfer to wire racks; cool completely. Roll or lightly dust cooled cookies with powdered sugar. Makes 3½ to 4 dozen cookies.

To Store: Place cookies in a single layer in an airtight container; cover. Store at room temperature for up to 3 days or in the freezer for up to 3 months.

Jingle Bell Wrap

Talk about a single-serving sensation! When giving just a few snowflake cookies, slip them into a plastic bag and secure with a super-cute tie. Knot a large jingle bell on each end of a length of ribbon and tie around the top of the bag.

Snowflake Cutout Cookies

Create a winter wonderland gift-giving theme with these gorgeous cookies decorated in Royal Icing, then accented with delicate white sprinkles in assorted designs, just as real snowflakes are.

½ cup butter
⅓ cup shortening
1 cup sugar
⅓ cup sour cream
1 egg
1 teaspoon vanilla
1 teaspoon finely shredded lemon peel
¼ teaspoon baking powder
½ teaspoon ground mace
¼ teaspoon baking soda
Dash salt
2½ cups all-purpose flour
1 recipe Royal Icing

1. In a large mixing bowl beat butter and shortening with an electric mixer on medium to high for 30 seconds. Add sugar, sour cream, egg, vanilla, lemon peel, baking powder, mace, baking soda, and salt. Beat until combined. Beat in as much of the flour as you can with the mixer. Stir in any remaining flour with a wooden spoon. Divide dough in half. Cover and chill for 1 to 2 hours or until easy to handle.
2. Preheat oven to 375°F. On a well-floured surface, roll each half of dough to a ⅛- to ¼-inch thickness. Using 2½- to 3-inch snowflake cutters dipped in flour, cut out dough. Use a wide spatula to place cutouts 1 inch apart on an ungreased cookie sheet.
3. Bake for 7 to 8 minutes or until edges are firm and bottoms are very light brown. Cool on wire racks. Frost with Royal Icing. Let dry. Makes 48 cookies.
To Store: Layer unfrosted cookies between sheets of waxed paper in an airtight container; cover. Store at room temperature for up to 3 days or freeze for up to 3 months. Thaw and decorate.

Royal Icing

Spread the pure white icing over the Snowflake Cutout Cookies. Once the icing dries to a smooth, hard matte finish, you're ready to begin piping. When not using, keep the icing covered with clear plastic wrap to prevent it from drying out.

1 16-ounce package powdered sugar (4½ cups)
3 tablespoons meringue powder*
¾ teaspoon cream of tartar
½ cup warm water
1 teaspoon vanilla

Macaroon Mix
Layering the mix in a jar looks pretty in itself. Add to it with a handwritten label, a chenille stem tie, and a circle of decorative paper trimming the lid.

1. In a medium mixing bowl combine powdered sugar, meringue powder, and cream of tartar. Add the warm water and vanilla. Beat with an electric mixer on low until combined. Beat on high speed for 7 to 10 minutes or until mixture is very stiff. Makes about 3 cups.
***Test Kitchen Tip:** Meringue powder is a mixture of pasteurized dried egg whites, sugar, and edible gums. Look for it in the baking aisle of your supermarket or at a specialty food store.

Christmas Macaroon Mix

This fun and colorful cookie makes a perfect gift for teachers, coaches, and youth leaders. Kids can help measure and layer the ingredients and create the labels.

1 7-ounce package flaked coconut (2⅔ cups)
⅔ cup sugar
½ cup chopped almonds, toasted
¼ cup all-purpose flour
¼ teaspoon salt
¼ cup chopped candied red and/or green cherries
2 tablespoons finely chopped candied orange peel

1. In a quart jar layer the coconut, sugar, almonds, flour, salt, candied cherries, and candied orange peel; fasten lid. Include directions for making macaroons. Makes 1 jar (enough for 30 cookies).
To Make Macaroons: Preheat oven to 325°F. Line cookie sheets with parchment paper or foil. Grease foil if using. In a bowl stir together the contents of the jar. Add 3 lightly beaten egg whites, stirring well to combine. Drop mixture by teaspoons 2 inches apart onto prepared cookie sheets. Bake for 15 to 18 minutes or until cookies are light brown. Transfer to a wire rack; cool. Makes 30 cookies.

Nature Jar

Give a glass or plastic jar a grand topper with natural elements accented with flowing ribbon. Hot-glue a small mound of pinecones to the top, along with a sprig of artificial greenery. Tie a ribbon bow, leaving long tails; hot-glue to one side.

Lemon-Ginger Snowballs

These tender lemon cookies look their holiday best rolled in coconut or white nonpareils. Tea, not a typical cookie ingredient, provides just the right mix of bright flavor and spice in these cookies.

½ cup shortening
1 tablespoon grated fresh ginger or finely chopped crystallized ginger
1 tablespoon vanilla
2 teaspoons honey-lemon-ginseng flavor green tea (from one 0.1-ounce tea bag)*
1 teaspoon finely shredded lemon peel
1 cup packed brown sugar
2 teaspoons ground ginger
1 teaspoon baking powder
½ teaspoon baking soda
¼ teaspoon salt
2 eggs
2½ cups all-purpose flour
Granulated sugar
Powdered Sugar Glaze
Coconut or white nonpareils

1. In a large mixing bowl beat shortening, ginger, vanilla, tea, and lemon peel on medium until fluffy. Add brown sugar; beat until well combined. Beat in ginger, baking powder, baking soda, and salt. Beat in eggs. Beat in as much of the flour as you can. Stir in any remaining flour. Refrigerate dough for 1 hour or until easy to handle.
2. Preheat oven to 350°F. Shape dough into 1-inch balls. Roll in granulated sugar and place on two ungreased baking sheets.
3. Bake for 10 minutes or until lightly browned. Cool for 2 minutes on baking sheets. Transfer to wire racks; cool completely. Dip in Powdered Sugar Glaze and coconut or white nonpareils. Place cookies on waxed paper and let dry. Makes 48 cookies.
Powdered Sugar Glaze: In a medium bowl combine 1 cup powdered sugar and 4 teaspoons water until glaze is a thick drizzling consistency.
***Test Kitchen Tip:** Cut open tea bag and add the loose tea to the batter. (Do not brew the tea.)

CHOCOLATE-RASPBERRY TASSIES

All Lined Up

What better way to separate cookies than to nestle them in a brand-new ornament box? First line the box with tissue, waxed paper, or parchment to cushion the treats.

Chocolate-Raspberry Tassies

The rich, gooey filling in these tarts has a hint of raspberry liqueur. Substitute your favorite liqueur or flavored syrup, or leave it out altogether.

Chocolate Pastry
6 ounces semisweet or bittersweet chocolate, chopped (1 cup)
2 tablespoons butter
1 egg, lightly beaten
¾ cup granulated sugar
1 tablespoon raspberry liqueur or raspberry-flavor syrup
2 teaspoons vanilla
Chocolate Buttercream (optional)

1. Prepare Chocolate Pastry. Preheat oven to 375°F. Shape pastry into 24 balls. Press each ball on bottoms and sides of 24 ungreased 1¾-inch muffin cups, using floured fingers if necessary; set aside.
2. For filling, in small saucepan heat and stir chocolate and butter over medium-low heat until melted and smooth. Remove from heat. Stir in egg, sugar, liqueur, and vanilla. Spoon 1 scant tablespoon filling in each pastry shell.
3. Bake for 12 to 15 minutes or until pastry is firm and filling is puffed. Cool in pans for 10 minutes. Run sharp thin-blade knife around tart edges; carefully remove from pans. Cool on a wire rack. If desired, pipe or spoon on a small amount of Chocolate Buttercream. Makes 24 tassies.
Chocolate Pastry: In a food processor combine 1¼ cups all-purpose flour, ⅓ cup sugar, ¼ cup unsweetened cocoa powder, and dash of salt; pulse to combine. Add ½ cup cold butter, cut up. Cover; process until crumbly. In small bowl whisk together 1 egg yolk and 2 tablespoons cold water. Add to processor; pulse until a dough ball forms (add water if dry). If needed, cover and refrigerate until easy to handle.
Chocolate Buttercream: In a medium mixing bowl beat ¼ cup softened butter on medium-high for 30 seconds. Gradually beat in 1 cup powdered sugar and 3 tablespoons unsweetened cocoa powder. Beat in 2 tablespoons milk. Gradually beat in 1 cup powdered sugar until piping consistency.
To Store: Place tassies in a single layer in an airtight container; cover. Store in the refrigerator for up to 3 days.

In-a-Twinkling

it's a wrap

Make a Scene

Create a winter wonderland atop a wrapped package. Use a few dots of hot glue to hold mini packages and bottlebrush trees clustered to one side. For detail, glue metallic beads to the trees for extra sparkle.

Big Bonus

A pair of thick yarns makes a pretty package tie. Wrap them around the box and knot it at the top, holding a loop of ribbon in place for the bow. Leave the ribbon tails long and tuck in a coordinating candy cane.

Initially Woven

Create a lovely woven effect by taping on three vertical ribbons. Weave through two horizontal ribbons and tape on the back. Instead of a tag, use a scrapbook letter to signify the initial of the gift recipient's first name.

Snow Gal

Paper doilies, left whole and trimmed, make a lacy snowlady body and head. Create the details by hot-gluing on buttons and snippets of ribbon. To make the face, use beads for eyes, sections of rubber washer for smile and eyebrows, and a tiny triangle of orange paper or crafts foam for the nose.

Jingle Bell Rock

To make this extra-special package trim, start with a length of decorative cording secured around the wrapped gift. Use hot glue to add a small snowflake ornament and top with a large jingle bell highlighting the center.

kids

Get in the spirit of the season from gift giving to decorating—with projects that will have the kids beaming.

Well-Dressed Friends

Make some new friends—literally—to bring you smiles all winter long.

Sparkle Snowmen

Use your imagination to trim these plump, glittery friends.

WHAT YOU NEED

Plastic foam balls
Table knife
White crepe paper streamer
Scissors
Decoupage medium
Small and medium paintbrushes; crafts glue
Toothpicks
Small and medium black round prong brads
Ribbon
Snowflake trims
Orange and other assorted colors of adhesive gems
Plastic lids, such as from laundry detergent
Trims, such as jingle bells, silk leaves, plastic ornaments, and chenille stems
Low-temp glue gun and glue sticks
Pliers (optional)
Large-flake white glitter

WHAT YOU DO

1. Cut off a sliver from the largest plastic foam ball so that the snowman will sit securely as shown in Photo A.

2. Cut short strips of streamer. Brush the foam ball with decoupage medium as shown in Photo B. Place a streamer strip on the decoupage medium and brush with another coat as shown in Photo C. Continue adding streamer strips to the ball in this manner, as shown in Photo D, until the entire rounded surface is covered. Cover the small foam ball in the same manner; allow decoupage medium to dry.

3. Coat paper-covered balls with a coat of decoupage medium and sprinkle with glitter as shown in Photo E. Let dry.

4. Place two toothpicks, ½ inch apart, into the the top of the snowman base as shown in Photo F. Press snowman head onto the toothpicks, placing crafts glue between the surfaces and pressing tightly together as shown in Photo G. Let dry.

5. Press prongs of brads into top foam ball to make face details as shown in Photo H. Press in a small brad for nose and adhere an orange gem to it.

6. Use low-temp glue to attach a lid for the hat. If there's an inner part to the cap that protrudes too far to place on snowman head, first snap off inner part of cap using pliers. Using the photos as inspiration, glue trims to hat. Coat hat with decoupage medium and sprinkle with glue. Let the glue dry.

7. Glue a snowflake "button" to each snowman; add a gem in the center. Tie a loose ribbon scarf around each neck.

Merry Mittens

Whatever your favorite designs, let them shine on clay mittens.

Cool Cutouts

WHAT YOU NEED

Oven-bake clay, such as Sculpey
Waxed paper; rolling pin
Mitten-shape cookie cutter
Straight and/or decorative-edge scissors
Toothpick and/or awl
Small straw; yarn

WHAT YOU DO

1. Unwrap clay and place between layers of waxed paper. Using a rolling pin, flatten clay until it is approximately ¼ inch thick. Peel off top layer of waxed paper as shown in Photo A.

2. Press the mitten cookie cutter into the clay as shown in Photo B. Pull away the excess as shown in Photo C. Decide on mitten design. Roll out clay between sheets of waxed paper and use straight or decorative-edge scissors to cut desired shapes as shown in Photo D.

3. Place shape onto mitten, using a toothpick to cut off edges that extend beyond mitten as shown in Photo E.

4. Use a toothpick or awl to press clay motifs into mitten, pressing in short lines as shown in Photo F or poking dots with the toothpick.

5. To make polka dots, roll small clay balls and press onto mitten as shown in Photo G. To secure, use a toothpick to press in spokelike designs on each circle. Add stripes as desired, pressing down clay with a toothpick as shown in Photo H.

6. Cut out a rolled cuff piece, fringing edge as shown in Photo I. Press it to mitten as shown in Photo J.

7. Flatten a clay ball to make a button; add stitch holes as shown in Photo K.

8. Make a stitched edge by poking holes with a toothpick as shown in Photo L. Use a straw to poke a hole through the upper right corner for a hanger.

9. Bake according to clay manufacturer's instructions. Let cool; thread hole with yarn for hanging.

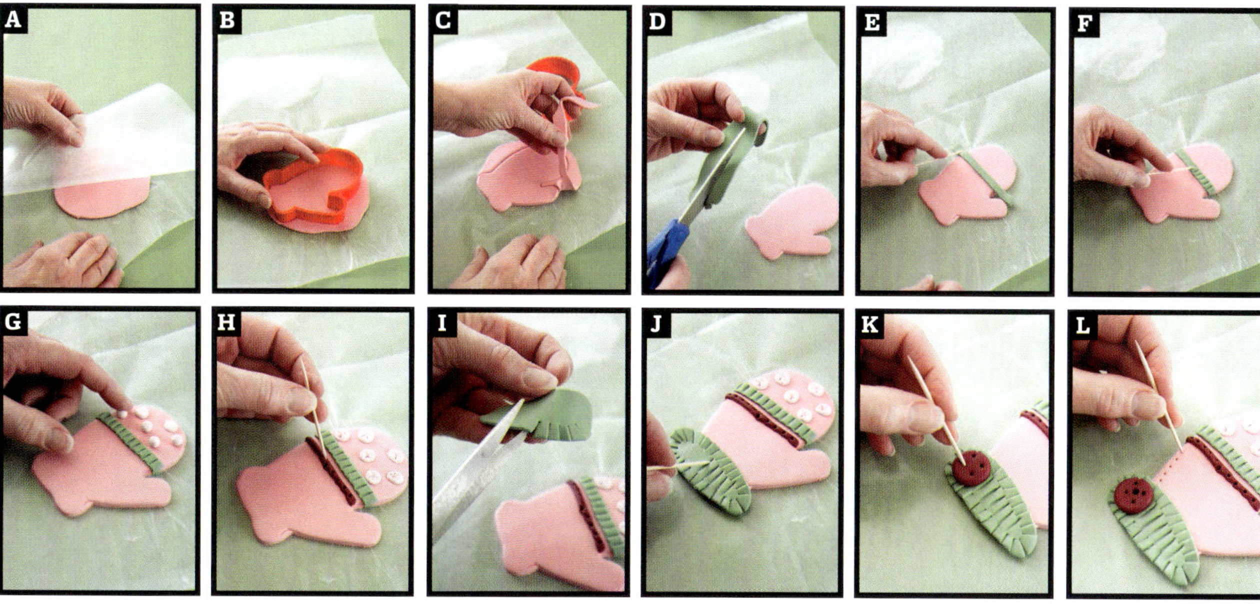

Pattern upon Pattern

Round and tissue-paper thin, cupcake liners work great for cutting fancy snowflakes. Flatten out the liner, then fold in half three times. Cut out a simple snowflake pattern, asking an adult for help if needed. Remember to keep some of the folded areas uncut so the snowflake doesn't fall apart. Open up and flatten, allowing an adult to iron the paper motif flat if desired.

Cute as Cupcakes

Patterned holiday cupcake liners make it easy for little ones to craft adorable decorations.

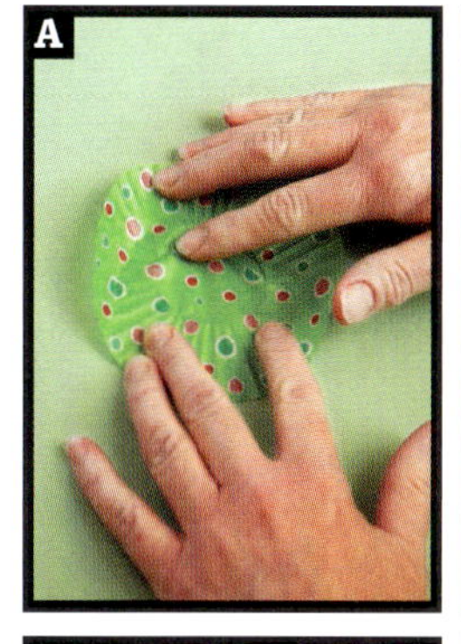
A

B

C

D

E

F

G

H

Santa's Cookie Plate

Have fun making a plate from which Santa can snatch his cookies. Using two colors of liners, flatten out two of one color and four of the other as shown in Photo A. Brush the back side of a clear round glass plate with a coat of glitter decoupage medium as shown in Photo B. Using one of the flattened cupcake liners, brush on a thin coat of decoupage medium as shown in Photo C and press it firmly to the plate center, smoothing out wrinkles with a paintbrush and more decoupage medium as shown in Photo D. Add four contrasting flattened liners evenly around the center, aligning the outer edges of the liners with the plate edge as shown in Photo E. Cut the remaining flattened liner into four even pie shapes as shown in Photo F. Add more decoupage medium to the uncovered areas of the plate back and use the pie- shape pieces to fill them in as shown in Photo G. Let dry. Use adhesive letters to spell "santa" on the plate top as shown in Photo H.

Mini Masterpieces

Encourage little Monets with super-fun splatter painting.

Season's Specklings

WHAT YOU NEED

Tracing paper
Pencil
Printer paper
Scissors
White cardstock
Painting apron
Old toothbrush
Metallic acrylic paints
Paper plate
¾- and 1-inch circle cutters
Glue stick
Frame

WHAT YOU DO

1. Trace the tree or snowman and scarf pattern(s) from page 158 onto tracing paper. Cut out the shape(s). Trace around the shapes onto printer paper and cut out as shown in Photo A.

2. On a well-covered work surface, open up the snowman shape or the background of the tree cutout and place on top of a piece of white cardstock. Put on an apron.

3. Place small amounts of paints on paper plate. Dip bristles of toothbrush into one paint color. Holding brush over pattern cutout, run thumb against toothbrush bristles to splatter paint onto card stock through pattern cutout as shown in Photo B for the tree or around the snowman shape to splatter-paint the background. Continue adding colors in this manner, washing and drying brush between colors, until desired look is achieved.

4. Carefully remove the pattern as shown in Photo C.

5. To make tree topper, cut a ¾-inch circle from splattered paper scrap as shown in Photo D. Glue on top of a 1-inch white circle. Glue at tip of treetop. Make scarf in the same manner. Trim around design to fit in frame. Insert in frame.

In-A-Twinkling bookmarks

Ribbon Beauty

Double up pretty ribbons for a lovely layered effect. Use embroidery floss and simple running stitches to hold the layers together. Sew a metal initial charm to the bookmark, topped with a dainty ribbon bow.

All-About-You Collage

Like a mini scrapbook page, papers, stickers, and punchouts combine to make a one-of-a-kind bookmark. Personalize it with a sentiment sticker and the reader's first initial.

Doodle It

Turn scribbles into a work of art. Scribble on a piece of white cardstock with a colored pencil. Pencil in some of the sections using various colors. Cut the colored work into a strip, then section off in three pieces as shown. Glue the pieces onto two paper backgrounds. Add the reader's initial to the bottom square with an adhesive letter.

Simply Classy

Perforated metallic silver paper lends a contemporary feel to this bookmark. Back it with a strip of solid cardstock, allowing a blank area at the bottom. Use hot glue to adhere a metal initial at the bottom of the strip.

So Circular

Emphasize a circular paper pattern with a pair of contrasting circles at the bottom of the bookmark. For the final polish, hot-glue an alphabet bead in the center of the circle. Back the entire bookmark with solid cardstock to make it firm and to frame the design.

Patterns

Place on fold

Place on fold

C B C B
A D A D

BERIBBONED TAG
& CHECK-IT-OUT WRAP
Cross Stitch
page 85

C B
A

SOCK FAVOR
Blanket Stitch
page 84

FINIAL FUN
page 29
Full-Size Pattern

SEASONAL
SYMBOL
page 31
Full-Size
Patterns

Place on fold

Place on fold

CARD CUT-UPS
STAR ORNAMENT
page 91
Full-Size Pattern
Placement Diagram

MEANINGFUL
MESSAGE
page 29
Full-Size Pattern

Place on fold

CARD CUT-UPS
STAR ORNAMENT
page 91
Enlarge 200%
Cut 5

Background Pattern

Inner Pattern

WELCOME FALL

POLKA-DOT PLAQUE
page 28
Enlarge 200%

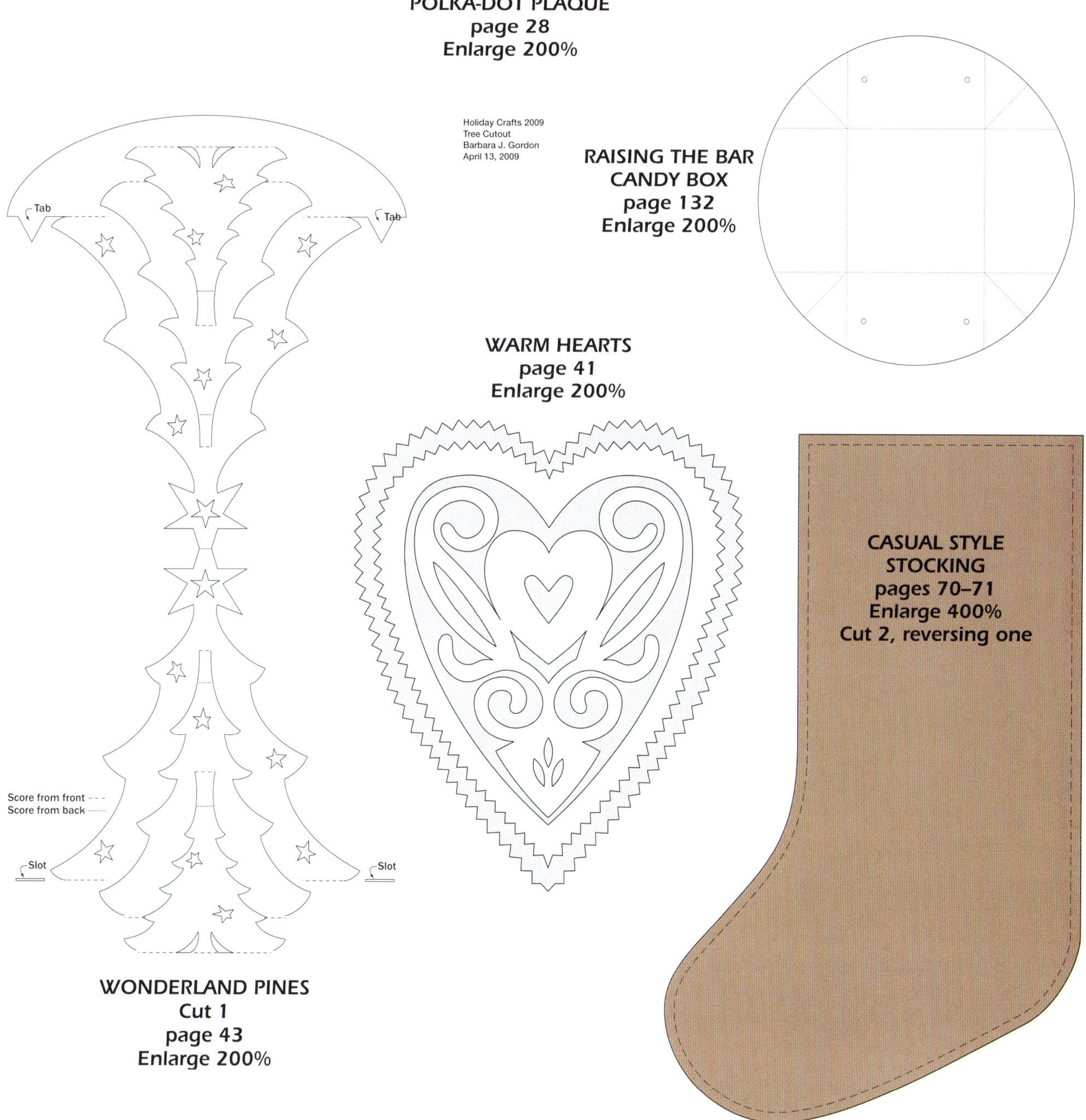

RAISING THE BAR CANDY BOX
page 132
Enlarge 200%

WARM HEARTS
page 41
Enlarge 200%

CASUAL STYLE STOCKING
pages 70–71
Enlarge 400%
Cut 2, reversing one

WONDERLAND PINES
Cut 1
page 43
Enlarge 200%

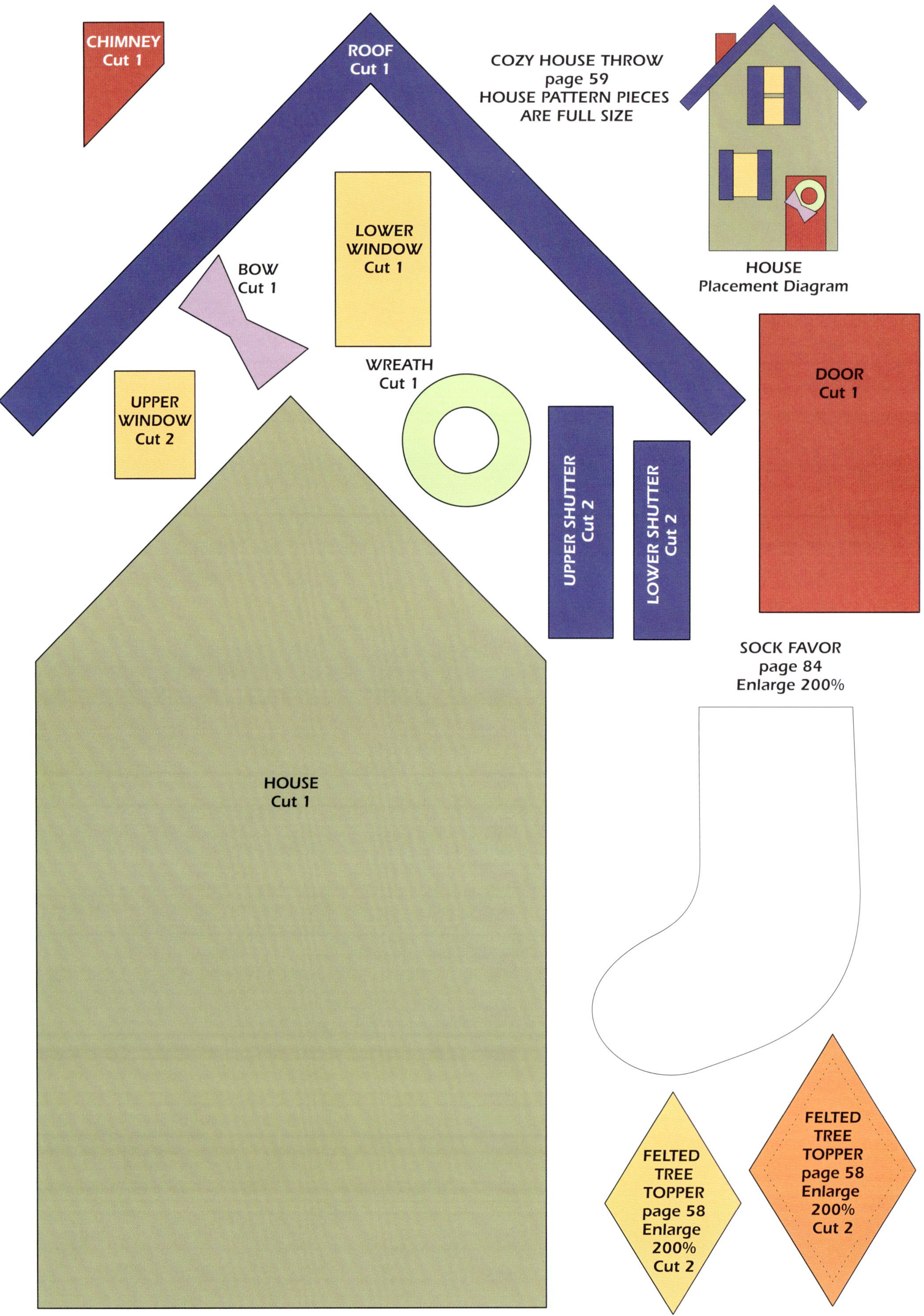
CHIMNEY
Cut 1
ROOF
Cut 1
COZY HOUSE THROW
page 59
HOUSE PATTERN PIECES
ARE FULL SIZE
HOUSE
Placement Diagram
LOWER
WINDOW
Cut 1
BOW
Cut 1
WREATH
Cut 1
UPPER
WINDOW
Cut 2
UPPER SHUTTER
Cut 2
LOWER SHUTTER
Cut 2
DOOR
Cut 1
SOCK FAVOR
page 84
Enlarge 200%
HOUSE
Cut 1
FELTED
TREE
TOPPER
page 58
Enlarge
200%
Cut 2
FELTED
TREE
TOPPER
page 58
Enlarge
200%
Cut 2

BOW DAZZLE
page 55
Enlarge 200%
Cut 2
O CHRISTMAS
TREE BACKGROUND
page 74
Enlarge 500%
MERRY MITTENS
pages 56–57
Enlarge 200%
Fold
WHO'S IT FROM
page 59
Enlarge 200%
Cut 1
WHO'S IT FROM
OWL WING
page 59
Enlarge 200%
Cut 2
O
CHRISTMAS
TREE
TREE 1
page 74
Enlarge 500%
TA-DA TOPPER
page 55
Enlarge 400%
Cut 1 each
Cut 5
STAR TOPPER
Placement Diagram
O
CHRISTMAS
TREE
TREE 2
page 74
Enlarge 500%
MERRY MUG
JAVA JESSIE
pages 130–131
Enlarge 200%

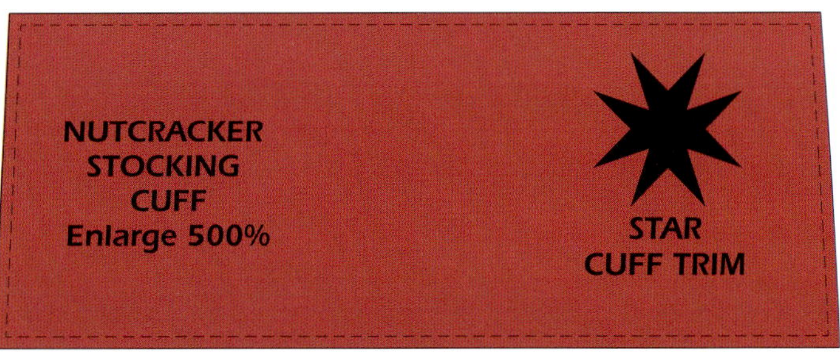

NUTCRACKER STOCKING
CUFF BAND Enlarge 500%

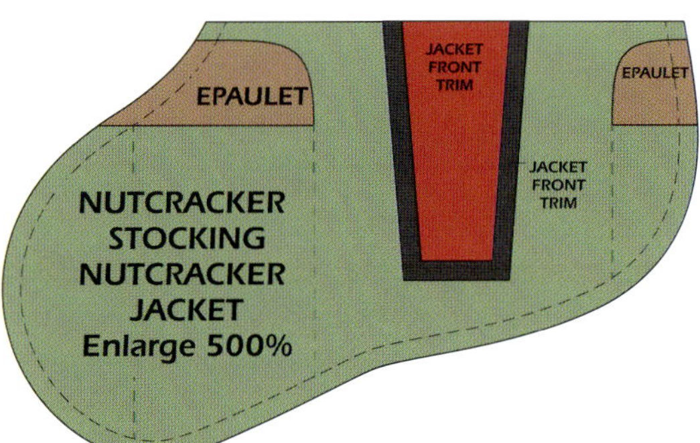

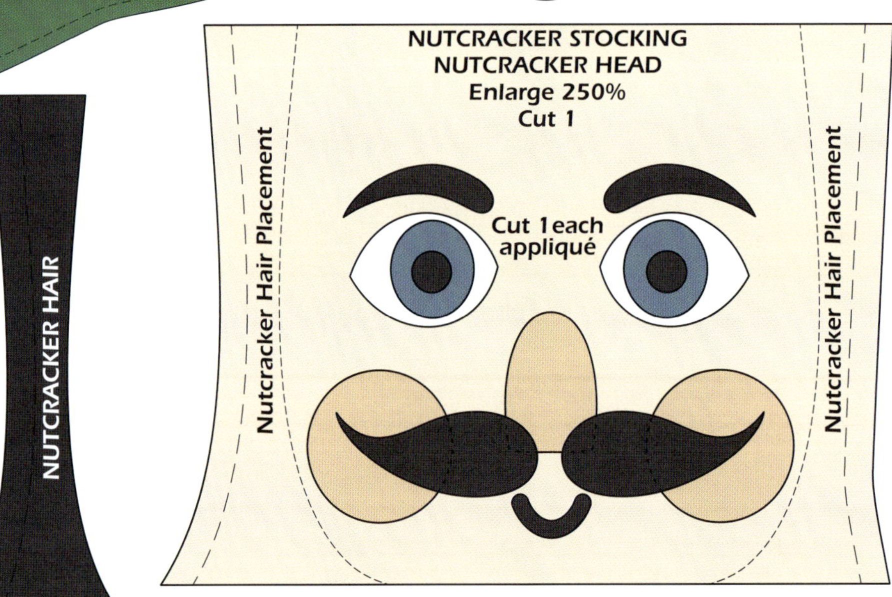

MINI MASTERPIECES

SNOWMAN
OUTER SCARF

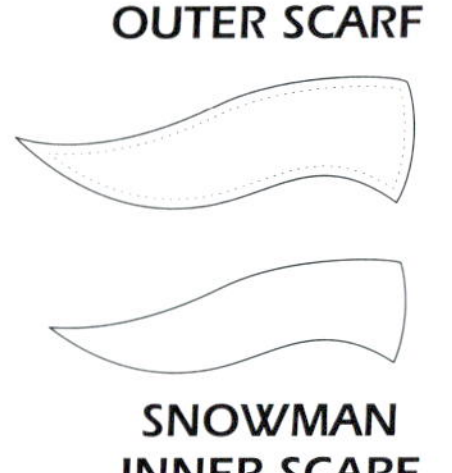

SNOWMAN
INNER SCARF

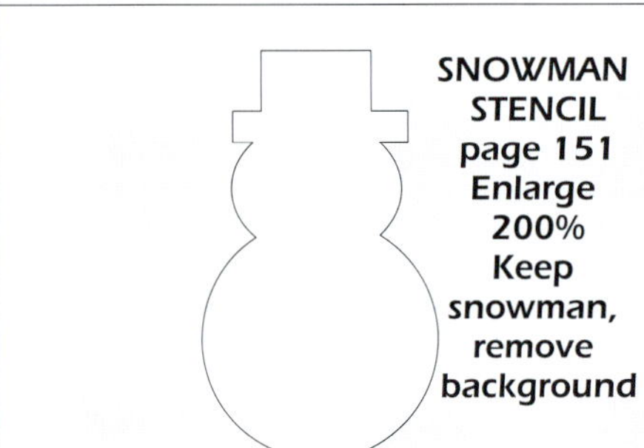

OUTER TREE
TOPPER

CENTER TREE
TOPPER

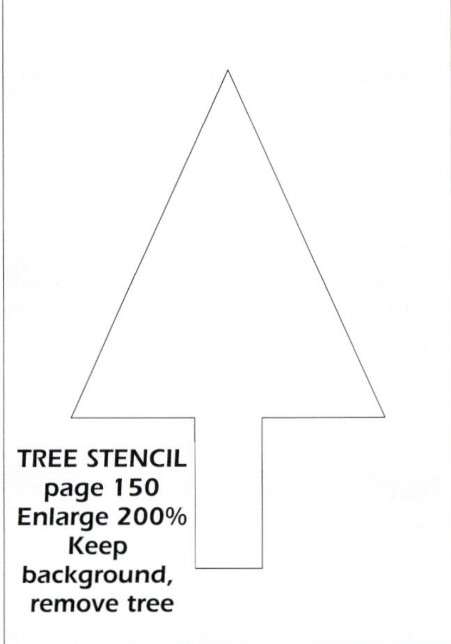

Index

DECORATING PROJECTS & GIFTS

index *continued*

RECIPES

CREDITS & SOURCES

PHOTO STYLING
Sue Banker and Catherine Brett

PHOTOGRAPHY
Karla Conrad
Jason Donnelly
Scott Little
Kritsada Panichgul
Jay Wilde

FOOD STYLISTS
Dianna Nolin
Jennifer Peterson

SOURCES
Pages 8–9: Stains and topcoats by General Finishes, 2462 Corporate Circle, East Troy, WI 53120; sales@generalfinishes.com.

Pages 26–29: Paints by Plaid Enterprises, Inc., PO Box 7600, Norcross, GA 30091-7600; plaidonline.com.

Page 52: Wool fabric by Weeks Dye Works, 1510-103 Mechanical Blvd., Garner, NC 27529; weeksdyeworks.com.

Pages 86–87: Paints by Plaid Enterprises, Inc., PO Box 7600, Norcross, GA 30091-7600; plaidonline.com.

Pages 144–145: Decoupage medium by Plaid Enterprises, Inc., PO Box 7600, Norcross, GA 30091-7600; plaidonline.com.

Pages 150–151: Paints by Plaid Enterprises, Inc., PO Box 7600, Norcross, GA 30091-7600; plaidonline.com.